PREFACE

Almost all idealists are inspired by their heroes, and they shape their identities by attempting to emulate the actions and behavior of those heroes. Naturally, depending on the person taken as a role model, emulation may have a positive or a negative effect on the devotee.

Looking at the issue from this perspective, it is possible to predict the character-development of a person who openly asserts the name of his hero.

Ali, the outstanding hero of the *futuwwa* spirit,[1] appears as a role model for all the self-sacrificing heroes awaited by the world of tomorrow. This brave figure was cultivated

---

[1] Derived from *fata'* (young man), the term *futuwwa* has become a symbol of rebellion against all evil and striving for sincere servanthood to God. As a term, *futuwwa* is a composite of virtues, such as benevolence, munificence, modesty, chastity, trustworthiness, loyalty, mercifulness, knowledge, humility and piety. It is, therefore, a fearless struggle against tyranny, and above all, it is love and mercy. It means placing other people above oneself, being generous and altruistic; it is self-denial, immunity to disappointment, and indulgence of other people's shortcomings. Considering all these aspects of this rich Arabic term, we can say that *futuwwa*, or chivalry, can best be summed up in the person of Ali ibn Abi Talib as he is one of the greatest representatives of the *futuwwa* spirit.

at the feet of the master of all masters. Not only was he a symbol of courage and gallantry, but he was also a leading figure in the depths of the metaphysical and spiritual worlds.

Even today, those who face the toughest challenges, calamities raining down upon them, will no longer need condolences. They will forget their troubles and burdens once they delved into the life of Ali, may God be pleased with him, to witness what he has endured.

Building new foundations in the name of righteousness and at a time where the ground has become rather slippery can only be achieved by those who possess his sagacity.

Here is the exemplary life story of this valiant role model…

AN EPISODE OF HIS HEROISM

Ali, may God be pleased with him, was the first person to pop into minds when bravery was mentioned amongst the Companions of the Prophet. He was hero that stood out in every battle he participated in, beginning with the Battle of Badr.[2]

When God Almighty revealed the verses testifying to the mortality of the Messenger of God like those who came before him and commanded his followers to stay on the right path after the Prophet's death, never turning back, it was Ali's voice that rose from among the early Muslim community: "I swear by God, since he is the one who has guided us onto divine path, we will never turn back. On his path, we shall fight to the death, even if he is martyred!"[3]

As destiny brought them all the way to the Battle of the Trench three years later, there was no change in his disposition and resolve. In contrast to previous battles, Prophet Muhammad, peace and blessings be upon him, had

---

[2] The Battle of Badr which took place at Badr, southwest of Medina, in the second year after the Hijrah (624 CE) was a decisive victory against the army of the polytheist Quraysh that was three times larger than that of the Muslims.

[3] Hakim, *Mustadrak*, 3/136 (4635).

changed his strategy of defense. He had ordered the digging of trenches around the city. His plan was to stop the enemy from reaching their lines. In spite of this, there were a few enemy soldiers who had managed to leap over the trenches. Amongst them was a man called Amr ibn Abdiwud. Those days, he was dubbed a man who had the power of a thousand men. Not only had he leaped over the trench, but he invited Muslims to a challenge, as he shouted: "Is there anyone amongst you who has the courage to face me!"

The young Ali, who was wearing armor, could not hold back anymore and asked for the permission of the noble Messenger: "Let me confront him, Oh Messenger of God!"

The Prophet knew that Amr was not an easy man to defeat, hence he replied: "This is Amr, so stay where you are!" Obviously, the Prophet was waiting for someone who could match Amr's strength and experience. However, Amr continued to provoke, as he shouted: "Is there not a man amongst you who has the courage to face me?" Then he added, "Where is the Paradise that you believe you would enter as martyrs?"

His intention was to intimidate the Muslims by demoralizing them. Ali's patience had run out. How could the voice of a non-believer have dominance upon the battle field? Once again, Ali turned towards the noble Messenger and said: "Let me confront him Oh Messenger of God!" However, the Prophet continued to instruct him to stay put.

By now, Ali had become quite restless. He wanted to put an end to Amr's arrogant insults as soon as possible. He could not hold himself back anymore, so he said: "Permit me to fight Oh noble Messenger, for I face two beautiful scenarios. If I defeat him, he will be sent to Hell, or if it is I who suffers defeat, I shall be sent to Paradise!"

This was a reflection of a robust faith. When necessary, one had to show that he was ready to die for the cause of God. However, his intention was not to become an easy prey for Amr. On the contrary, his prime goal was to send Amr where he belonged.

Amr, on the other hand, was having quite a time. His confidence grew by the minute since there was no one around to accept his challenge. He recited poems with implications of insults and taunted the Muslims with his degrading words.

Such insolence had to be dealt with in a way it deserved. Once again, Ali roared like a lion, asking for permission. Alas, the Messenger's reply was no different. "That is Amr!" said the noble Messenger, as he cautioned Ali, reminding him about the reputation of his opponent.

Nevertheless, Ali had already made up his mind. According to him, no one had the right to act in such manner in the presence of the noble Messenger. Those who dared had to be punished accordingly so that a message would be sent to future culprits. This time, Ali stood up and implored: "Even if he is Amr, permit me to fight Oh Messenger of God!"

Perhaps, Ali's faith was strong enough to overcome Amr's strength. Therefore, the noble Messenger gave in to his persistence and granted him permission.

Ali wasted no time, as he stood face to face with Amr. Amr asked who he was and upon hearing Ali's identity, he became more impudent, shouting in an intimidating manner: "Oh the sons of Manaf![4] Oh the son of my brother! Couldn't they find someone older amongst your uncles to challenge me? I will take no pleasure in spilling your blood." Ali's reply came quickly: "I have no problem spilling your blood!"

Words were magical in essence, and Ali wished to utilize them in a most efficient way. He had successfully made his initial move. Amr, on the other hand, fumed with rage. Quickly, he began to swing his sword. His blows came so rapidly that sparks flew from Ali's shield each time his sword made contact.

However, this time Amr's opponent was Ali, the Gallant Lion. Unexpectedly and to everyone's surprise, Ali had defeated Amr with a striking move. They all stared at each other with shock on their faces. The lifeless body of the legendary Amr had fallen to the ground. Who could stand before this young man who defeated Amr with ease? As Muslims began to chant *Allahu Akbar* (God is the All-Great,) the noble Messenger displayed a sigh of relief. Ali

---

[4]   The sons of Manaf were the descendants of Abdi Manaf, who was the great great grandfather of the Prophet and the leader of the Quraysh—the most important tribe in Mecca.

had finally sent Amr to the eternal place Allah had appointed for him, and no one doubted this. The news that came with the words *Allahu Akbar* was patiently awaited by all those who were praying for victory. Ali was smiling as he approached the noble Messenger. Upon seeing this, Umar ibn Khattab said: "Why didn't you take his armor? No one amongst the Arabs has a finer armor." "I felt ashamed to strip him of his armor," replied Ali.

Who was Ali, this unique hero of the soul of benevolence? Where was he raised, and what sort of upbringing did he have? What were the dynamics that formed Ali? What sort of a future did destiny have in store for him? Let us now analyze his life story and discover what made him a role model for all of us...

THE ENVIRONMENT IN WHICH
HE WAS RAISED

His father's name was Abdi Manaf ibn Abdul Muttalib (Abu Talib), and his mother was Fatima bint Asad. He was born in the Ka'ba thirty years after the Elephant Incident.[5] His grandfather, Abdul Muttalib was one of the most respected chieftains of Mecca. The Muttalib family presented a picture of unity with Ka'ba. Perhaps, this is why he was the first and only child who was born in Ka'ba. No one before or after him was to be credited with such honor.

His mother thought "Haydar" which meant "The Lion", would be the most appropriate name for him, but his father Abu Talib called him Ali. Abu Talib was the Prophet's biological uncle. The Prophet's father had died before Muhammad, peace and blessings be upon him, was born, followed by his mother when he was only six. Young Muhammad was an orphan now, and according to his grandfather Abdul Muttalib's will, he was to be raised

---

5   Since the army of Abraha, the Abyssinian ruler of Yemen, brought some elephants with them to attack the Ka'ba in the year 571 CE, their campaign came to be known as the Elephant Incident, which is commonly used as a marker in Arab history.

by his uncle Abu Talib. For this reason, they lived in the same house. Prior to his death, Abdul Muttalib had pulled his son Abu Talib aside and said, "Oh Abu Talib! You see this son of mine, his status is very important. Do not allow for even the smallest harm to reach him."[6]

Many years had gone by, and the most trusted of human beings had grown up. He would join his uncle on trade journeys now. This was the way that he met Khadija and married her. Following his marriage to Khadija, the noble Messenger moved out of Abu Talib's house, but he was a man of loyalty, so he frequently visited his uncle's house to ask if the family needed anything. It was around this time when Abu Talib's younger son Ali was born.

This was the period of scarcity in Mecca, and Abu Talib's family was also affected by the shortage of rations. They were going through tough times, and the noble Prophet, peace and blessings be upon him, felt deeply concerned about their situation. In order to look for a solution, he went to his other uncle Abbas and said: "Why don't you take responsibility for one of his children and I for the others."

The Prophet's compassionate solution was quite logical, and Abbas gladly accepted the offer. Quickly, they went to Abu Talib, and together they convinced him to accept their proposal. Abu Talib became quite emotional with his nephew's sensitive offer as he remembered the day he had came to his house as an orphan. He realized

---

6   Ibn Kathir, *al-Bidaya wa'n-Nihaya*, 2/281.

how accurate his decision was when amongst all the brothers; he was the one who had taken responsibility of young Muhammad. He said that Ali's elder brother, Aqil can remain with him, but they could take responsibility over the others. Ja'far was taken by Abbas, and Ali went with Muhammad, peace and blessings be upon him. At the time, Ali was only five years old.[7]

From that day on, Ali was under the supervision of the noble Prophet. He was raised by the manners of the noble Messenger in a companionship that would last for five years, until the day Muhammad, peace and blessings be upon him, was given the mission of Prophethood. This togetherness also protected Ali from the filth of ignorance and prepared him as a guide to a life of purity. In fact, Ali was one of the few people who opened his eyes to Islam at such a tender age. Indeed, he was raised by the Chosen Messenger who himself received his manners from the All-Merciful and the All-Compassionate. In this pure environment, Ali was protected from the negatives of the age of ignorance, enabling him to develop a will power as tough as granite. Ali's foundation was quite solid, but many challenging tasks and demanding situations awaited young Ali.

---

[7]   Haythami, *Majmau'z-Zawaid*, 8/153.

ALI'S EMBRACE OF ISLAM AND
HIS CHIVALROUS SPIRIT

The eternal sun had risen from the cave of Hira on top of the Mount of Light to brighten the universe, and its initial rays descended upon Mecca. Obviously, the noble Messenger's primary ally would be Khadija as she was the first person to embrace the divine light. The excitement occurring in the home of Muhammad the Trustworthy and the frequent visits to Waraqa ibn Nawfal was an indication that something innovative was developing. Young Ali was also aware of these changes as he watched them perform the prayers with curious eyes. He was only ten at the time. First he asked what they were doing, and the Messenger of God replied: "I am performing the prayer (*Salah*) for the Lord of the worlds."

This was the first time Ali had heard of such a thing. Once again, he asked attentively, "Who is the Lord of the worlds?"

The noble Messenger of God sat Ali on his lap, and like a compassionate father, he began to explain his experience on the Mount of Light (Jabal an-Nur) and how he was given the mission of Prophethood. Then the noble Proph-

et added: "He is the One and only Allah. He has no part-
ners. He has created all beings and provides their suste-
nance. Everything is in His powerful grasp. It is He who
creates life and death. He is the All-Powerful who possess-
es the power to do anything."

These were the words of a compassionate fatherly figure,
and they were spoken directly into the heart of young Ali.
He trusted the Prophet so much that he would not even
hesitate to walk towards death with him. However, this
was an important decision, so he felt the need to consult
his father. In any case, a father's place was inimitable. The
noble Prophet also had a request; he advised Ali not to tell
anyone else about their conversation.

That night, Ali thought about the whole issue and
argued in his mind, "Why do I need to consult my par-
ents over such an important matter as belief in God?"
Finally, he had made his mind up. As the morning sun
rose above Mecca, he went to God's Messenger and said,
"What did you explain to me yesterday and what is your
invitation?"

Perhaps Ali was experiencing maturity at such a tender
age by deciding to make his own mind up without con-
sulting his father. This would include him into the exclu-
sive few who had embraced Islam first. The noble Messenger instructed him to sit beside him and invited Ali to
declare the *Shahada*, or testimony of faith. Young Ali,
who was at the tender age of ten when the first revelations
came down, became the first person following Khadija to

accept Islam. He had recited the *Kalima at-Tawhid* by say-ing *La ilaha illallah Muhammadun rasulullah*, which means "There is no deity other than God, and Muham-mad is the Messenger of God" even before his elders and believed in the All-Merciful and the All-Compassionate with his own free will.[8] In any case, how could he refrain from faith, living in a house where the sound of divine Revelation echoed constantly and the future plans in the name of Islam were drawn on the walls that trembled with divine Revelations?

From that point on, young Ali would never leave the side of his uncle's son Muhammad, the Messenger of God. He wished to be the first to hear the divine Revelations as they came down and flowed from the lips of the noble Messenger. As the noble Messenger extensively used the house of Ibn Arqam[9] for religious gatherings, Ali went with him to become a regular member of the new com-munity. An important duty awaited Ali now. He was to bring news of the developments occurring outside while he competed with others in educating himself with divine Revelations as well. With each passing day, a new face would dive into the pool of faith, purified of all ignorance to be included in the ranks of faith.

---

[8]   Ibn Abdil Barr, *al-Istiab*, 3/1090.

[9]   Ibn Arqam, one of the Prophet's young Companions, offered his house in Mecca to be used for religious gatherings of the Prophet where he taught his small band of Companions, recited them the Revelations and led the prayers in congregation for several years during which believers were being closely watched and harassed by the polytheist Quraysh to stop the spread of Islam.

Ali seemed like the twin of the master of all masters... He had become one with the Prophet so much so that during one occasion when they distressed him, Ali shouted with anger: "You may ask me whatever you wish...As much as you wish...Ask me anything from the Book of Allah..! By Allah, I know very well which verse came down for what reason, where, and when!"[10]

He was the foremost student of the noble Messenger and the leading pupil of the holy Qur'an. Many greats had fallen behind in the race towards Islam, and Ali became a guide to those who came after.

Abu Talib was a tolerant father, and he had total confidence in his nephew, Muhammad the Trustworthy. One day, he had seen Ali perform the prayer behind the Prophet. He knew about the Revelations received by his nephew and his months of seclusion on the Mount of Light, but he had no knowledge of Ali's pledge to Muhammad, peace and blessings be upon him. At first he preferred to remain silent for a while but young Ali was quick to use his brilliance. Assuming that his father may jump to conclusions, he rushed to him upon the completion of his prayer and said, "Oh my dear father!"

The tone of his voice was velvety and sensitive as he continued, "I believe in God and His Messenger. Father, I...I pledge to follow Muhammad."

Abu Talib would have never given consent to such a change if he had not known his nephew Muhammad so

---

10 Mizzi, *Tahzibu'l-Kamal*, 20/487.

well. However, the person his son chose to follow was no other than Muhammad, peace and blessings be upon him. Therefore, he replied: "Continue on your path my son, for he will only call you to good!"[11]

On another occasion, Ali stood behind the Prophet to perform the prayer. Upon seeing this, Abu Talib turned to his other son Ja'far and said: "Go my son, stand behind your uncle's son and perform the prayer!"[12]

Not long after, they were joined by another person who was blessed with the opportunity of growing up in the Prophet's house. He was a young slave who had been emancipated by the noble Messenger. He was Zayd ibn Haritha, and not only was he liberated by the Prophet, but he was also raised to the level of masters. Those around the Prophet were young but they represented the spirit of chivalrous heroism. Every one of them was dedicated to convey his message throughout Mecca. As the noble Messenger spoke to Ali and Zayd, who lived with him, he was preparing them for the challenging days ahead. He wanted to educate them as problem solving heroes of the future.

Indeed, Ali was a Muslim now, but in those days embracing Islam brought along many difficulties, and Ali was well aware of this. They were closely monitored by the polytheist Quraysh and were followed every step of the way. Wherever they went, whoever they spoke to,

---

[11] Ibn Hisham, *as-Siratu'n-Nabawiyya*, 2/86.
[12] Dhahabi, *Mizanu'l-I'tidal*, 3/355.

there would be a pair of eyes watching them. Anyone who interacted with them would be approached and spoken to. The disbelievers used false excuses and lies to deviate people from embracing Islam.

Abu Dharr, from the Ghifari tribe that lived in the Waddan valley outside Mecca, had heard of the changes in Mecca. One day, his curiosity brought him all the way to the Ka'ba. Since he was aware of the delicate circumstances, he abstained from talking to anyone. He decided to wait in the Ka'ba hoping that Muhammad would come there. On the third day, Ali approached him and stealthily asked the reason for his visit. After realizing his intention and seeing the sincerity on his face, Ali said: "Without doubt, Muhammad, peace and blessings be upon him, is genuine. He is the Messenger of God. When you wake up tomorrow morning, follow me but keep your distance. If I sense danger, I will stop, you continue walking. However, if we do not run into any problems follow me all the way."[13] This was the way Ali had guided Abu Dharr to the path of faith.

Zayd and Ali were like the hands and feet of the noble Messenger. They were like moths around the light as they ran circles around the Prophet. They were running their hearts out as they tried to invite people to the right path. On some occasions, they would invite people to dinner and support the Prophet as he explained Islam to his guests. God knows how many times they had organized a

---

[13] Tabarani, *al-Mu'jamu'l-Awsat*, 3/109 (2633).

feast at the skirts of Mt. Qubays where God's Messenger had invited people to Islam!

The method of invitation was sincere and kind, the request was quite simple, and the person who invited them was the trustworthy one, yet their hearts were hardened, and the essence of their disposition was dire. All he wanted from them was two words (*Kalima at-Tawhid*). They were easy to pronounce, yet they weighed extremely heavy on the *mizan*, or the divine scales of justice. All they had to do was to say these two words, and their eternal life would have been salvaged. The blessings of both realms were through this path, and one had to be a devoted supporter, an unyielding protector, and a sincere friend to attain them. The Messenger of God was constantly looking for such upstanding individuals. Whenever he reminded people of this request, although Ali was the youngest in the assembly, he always stood up, and placing his hand on his chest, he would shout: "I am here Oh God's Messenger!"

On most occasions, the Prophet would repeat himself by asking Ali to sit down. However, he always hoped that Ali's support would be an example to others.[14]

Ali was an intelligent, valiant young man. He carefully planned all his moves. He did not act upon anything before calculating and estimating the result. This is why the noble Messenger discussed matters with him quite often. On the day of Taif when the Prophet decided to

---

[14] Ibn Hanbal, *Musnad*, 1/159 (1371).

travel there in hopes of finding hearts open to his message, he called Ali for a lengthy consultation. Displeased by this, some would even speak their minds regarding the matter. The words spoken eventually reached the ears of the noble Prophet, who then took control of the matter by stating, "The private consultation I had with Ali was not my choice; it was the will of Allah."[15]

With this statement, he pointed to the real decision maker. He was actually teaching them that every step taken and every decision made were within the knowledge and approval of God Almighty.

---

[15] Ibn Kathir, *al-Bidaya wa'n-Nihaya*, 7/357.

THIRD PERIOD OF PROTECTION

Hearts hardened with polytheism were not pleased with the new developments. With each day passing by, they were taking a sturdier stand against the Divine Light that emerged from the Mount of Light. It was the third term of protection, and once again Ali's father Abu Talib took responsibility of protecting the noble Messenger from the malice of the Quraysh. He protected him during the delicate period in which the noble Messenger was given the mission of Prophethood just as he did when he was an orphan child. Abu Talib took extreme care so that no harm would come to him. In any case, how could he have refused such a responsibility? Muhammad, peace and blessings be upon him, was entrusted to him by his own father, Abdul Muttalib. He strongly believed that it was his duty to protect the Prophet, peace and blessings be upon him.

The number of believers was gradually increasing, yet there was no smile on Ali's pale face. The reason for this was that every day he witnessed people accepting the faith, yet his own father and mother had not embraced Islam. He was deprived of sleep, thinking about the fact that he could not touch the hearts of his closest family members. There was nothing he could do because the Prophet had

explained Islam to his father many times without success.
Perhaps, it was not yet the right time.

Conditions in Mecca had worsened. They had tried to
get support from the town of Taif yet there was no sympa-
thy there either. Each day the problems increased. One day
the Quraysh closed the gates of Mecca to all believers, evict-
ing them from the city. This was a life in exile which would
last for three years..! The Quraysh, who fed on ignorance,
was committing the biggest shame of humanity by con-
demning innocent people, including children, to famine
and starvation in the desert. They were abandoned and left
face to face with death. This life in exile and deprivation
lasted a grueling three years in pain and suffering.[16] Only
those who experienced it could understand the enormity of
this tormenting ordeal. Apparently, the decision to exile the

---

[16] As the number of the people who believed increased, the chieftains
of the Quraysh became more alarmed and began to see Islam as a
threat to the entire life of the city of Mecca. The hatred and animos-
ity from those who ran the city reached such a level that they could
not tolerate the existence of the Prophet and the small band of believers and would not rest until they were "cleansed" from the city.
However, they could not dare to kill the Prophet because of the
protection of Abu Talib, who took the pledge to save his nephew
from harm with the help of all his relatives and the Muslims. Since
the Quraysh could not get rid of the Prophet, they decided to cut all
ties with the believers, allowed no one to trade with them and cut off
all sources of goods, food, and water. Due to this severe boycott, the
believers formed a refugee camp of sorts outside Mecca, in a place
called Shib Abi Talib. The Prophet and his followers were cast out in
the open in the silent, deadly conditions of the desert days and nights
so that they would die of hunger and thirst, without the need for
feuds which could last for centuries.

Muslims had been a unanimous one. They documented their ruling of tyranny in point form and brazenly hung it on the wall of the Ka'ba as if they were acting in a virtuous manner. Moreover, they barricaded all roads to prevent people from helping those in exile.

The believers who were already experiencing great hardship and destitution underwent additional pain and suffering. First, Ali's father Abu Talib passed away. In spite of the Prophet's persistence, he died without embracing the faith. He left without leaving anything of value to his son Ali. This was an unbearable pain for the gallant lion who risked everything in the name of faith.

Three days had not gone by since the death of his father, and Khadija, a woman he loved like a mother, also passed away. She was a source of condolence for them. Ali experienced the pain of the loss of another fortress who he could sincerely call, "Mother!" Not long ago, she was one of the wealthiest women in Mecca. Ali had competed with Zayd to invite people to banquets prepared by her. Now, the same Khadija, who had sacrificed her wealth on the way of God and much of what she still owned was seized after this boycott, had closed her eyes to this world, and this occurred during the days of great suffering and tormenting exile.[17]

The only condolence for Ali was his mother Fatima's embrace of Islam following the death of her husband. For

---

[17] This year is called the "Year of Sorrow" since Abu Talib, the Prophet's greatest protector, and his beloved wife Khadija, the first comforter and helper of the Prophet, passed away in this year.

a brief moment, he forgot his troubles and felt joy. Who would not be happy to witness their mother's conversion to Islam?

Contrary to all difficulties, Ali knew that he needed to show patience. The significance of patience in faith could be compared to the significance of the head to the human body. The faith of those who had no patience was in jeopardy. Now was the time to act, not to judge because deeds had to be performed before the Day of Judgment arrived.

Everyone who came to offer their condolences had pale faces. He could see that they were all suffering together and feeling the same pain. During these difficult days amongst the dust and dirt, Ali's faith was strengthened and reinforced like iron. Many years later, when he found a little comfort, he would remember the days when the first Companions wept until their garments were soaked with tears. He would constantly express his longing for those days as he advised others. On one occasion he said: "Be the fountain of knowledge and the light of the night; carry old clothes but always possess a new heart. This is the way you will always be remembered with commemorations in this world."[18]

---

[18]　Abu Nuaym, *Hilyatu'l-Awliya*, 1/77.

ALI'S MISSION DURING THE
GREAT MIGRATION

The deaths of Abu Talib and Khadija had boosted the confidence of the Quraysh. They constantly strived to produce fiendish plans. They had heard of rumors regarding mass migration and feared that the Messenger of God would also leave Mecca. They needed to come up with a plan before it was too late. Finally, the chieftains of Mecca gathered at the Dar'un Nadwa, the committee where important decisions were made. The committee members proposed different solutions to the matter, but a man that they had not seen before (Satan) kept on refusing, suggesting that none of the proposals would solve the problem. He argued that the solution should remove the problem from its roots.

Finally, it was Abu Jahl's proposal that got the approval of the entire committee. He suggested: "We should kill him. To avoid bloodshed amongst our tribes, let us select a young man from each tribe and get them to attack Muhammad at once. This way we can stop Banu Hashim[19]

---

[19] Banu Hashim, or the children of Hashim, is the branch of Quraysh to which the Prophet belonged. Hashim was the Prophet's great grandfather and the son of Abdu Manaf. He organized the trade caravans to the north and the south of Arabia, and Mecca grew rich during his leadership.

from seeking revenge." Satan in disguise of a strange old man also concurred with the decision. They were unanimous on their verdict to kill the Messenger whom they had given the title of "The Trustworthy One." The Prophet would be assassinated through an ambush which would be executed during the night.

Little did they know that no scenario planned on earth would be permitted to take stage unless it had the approval of the heavens, and this is exactly what happened.

The Divine permission had come, and the noble Messenger of God, accompanied by Abu Bakr, intended to migrate to Medina. However, before they left, there were some important matters which needed urgent attention. He called the young valiant Ali and explained thoroughly what needed to be done after they had departed from Mecca. Ali was to fulfill his duty and then meet them in Medina.

The primary imperative issue was to make sure that the Quraysh does not obtain any information regarding the migration. The Quraysh were to be misled into believing that the Prophet was still in his home. For this reason, Ali would stay at the Prophet's house that night to confront whatever they had planned against the Prophet. The noble Prophet assured him and said that they would not even be able to harm a hair on his body.

Ali wore the Prophet's garment and lied on his bed. He thought to himself, if anyone needed to be sacrificed for this holy mission, it should be him who submits to the will of God, just as Ishmael, peace be upon him, who lay under Abraham's knife. He felt no fear, especially after the sultan of hearts spoke to him: "Wrap yourself in my green cloak and remain there. By the will of Allah, no harm shall come to you."[20]

At the time Ali was twenty three. That night, the Quraysh decided to execute their plan. The Prophet's house came under siege. The group of young assassins quickly raided the house and rushed in. However, their plan failed. By this time the noble Messenger had already made his way to Mount Sawr in the southeast of Mecca.

It was their turn to panic as they asked in shock, "Where is your master?"

They were never going to get anything out of Ali. Under intense pressure all he would say was this: "You wanted to expel him from Mecca…so he went!"[21]

There was also the matter of valuables entrusted to Muhammad the Trustworthy for safe-keeping; everything that was entrusted to him had to be returned to their rightful owners. What kind of a trust was this which compelled them to give their most valuable possessions for safe-keeping to a person whom they made all sorts of plans to kill? He was an inimitable trustee who would protect the valuables of those who wished to kill him even if it meant risking the life of his beloved Ali. For the next three days, Ali distributed the valuables that the noble Prophet had in safe-keeping. When he had successfully completed his mission,

20 Ibn Hisham, *as-Siratu'n-Nabawiyya*, 3/5.
21 Tabari, *Tarikhu'l-Umam wa'l-Muluk*, 1/568.

the time for Ali's migration also arrived. His mother, a few friends, and his future wife Fatima, the daughter of the noble Messenger, peace and blessings be upon him, accompanied him on this journey.

Although they left Mecca a few days after the Prophet, they planned to meet up with him at Quba in Medina. The noble Prophet and Abu Bakr stayed in a cave on Mount Sawr in the southeast of Mecca for a few days to make sure that it was safe to travel the rest of the way. Ali had rushed all the way so that he could catch up with the Prophet as planned. He had been walking so vigorously that his feet were swollen and had blisters all over them. As they made it to Quba, Ali was not in a condition to walk anymore. The noble Messenger asked: "Where is Ali, bring him to me at once." "Oh the Messenger of God, he is in no condition to walk!" they said.

The compassionate Prophet quickly went next to Ali and saw the condition of his feet. The Prophet of mercy could not hold his tears upon taking a glance at Ali's feet. Ali was in pain, covered in blisters. The noble Prophet applied his sanctified saliva on Ali's sores. As all those present witnessed a miracle in the making, Ali's feet were healed instantly. He never had problems with his feet for the rest of his life.

THE MESSENGER OF GOD DECLARES
ALI AS A BROTHER

When they reached Medina, God's Messenger decided to declare each immigrant, called *Muhajir*, as a brother to a Muslim of Medina, called *Ansar*, or Helper. Everyone was paired up as brothers, yet there was no one left to pair with Ali. Ali felt so miserable about the whole issue that he expressed his feelings to the noble Prophet, peace and blessings be upon him. The gallant lion was weeping vociferously like a child. Moreover, he was openly displaying his disappointment to the Prophet, as he said: "You declared everyone as brothers, yet I have no brother."

Little that he knew, he would be the most fortunate out of all. His declared brother would be the most trusted of all human beings, the Messenger of Allah. First, the noble Messenger consoled him; he placed his hand on Ali's shoulder and hugged him. Then, in front of everyone, he said: "Oh Ali! I am your brother in this world and in the life after."

Suddenly, all of Ali's worries had disappeared; he was a man envied by everyone now. How could you not envy him? In addition to the many virtues he possessed, he was also declared a brother to the Prophet now.[22]

---

[22] Ibn Sa'd, *Tabaqatu'l-Kubra*, 3/21.

THE LION OF BADR

The vengeful enmity of the idol worshippers seemed to be never ending. Vigorously, they made plans to destroy the Muslims whom they had let slip through the palm of their hands during the Migration in 622 CE. Finally, their paths crossed at Badr. Until that particular day, permission to fight had not been granted by the Almighty; the Muslims had been forced to restrict themselves. At last, the permission had come, and the days of defense-only were over. Although, technically they would still be defending themselves, this time, however, it would be on a battle field.

The two armies met near the wells of Badr. Ali, may God be pleased with him, was amongst the few men who engaged in combat first. With an incredible speed, Ali made his move, and Walid the enemy of God fell to the ground. Ali's triumph boosted the moral of the army that was fortified with divine blessing.

The Messenger of God loved Ali so much that even when he sent him away to battles at distant lands, he would remember his cousin and pray to the All-Merciful on his behalf: "Oh Allah! Do not collect my soul before I behold Ali again!"

One day as the Prophet sat down, leaning to the walls of Medina, he was informed that the person following Abu Bakr and Umar, may God be pleased with them, would also be blessed with Paradise. Suddenly he heard footsteps, and realizing that someone was approaching, he prayed: "Oh Allah! By your will, let it be Ali!"

The Prophet had wished paradise for Ali, and indeed the person coming was Ali, the son of Abu Talib.[23] The Prophet presented Ali his own sword which he named Zulfiqar. Ali would keep this sword like a sacred trust throughout his life and gain victories with the blessings of the Zulfiqar.

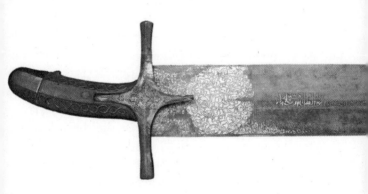

Sword of Ali ibn Abi Talib
Topkapi Palace Museum, Inventory no. 21/138

---

[23] Ibn Abi Shayba, *Musannaf*, 6/351 (31952).

ALI AT UHUD

The Quraysh had suffered a crushing defeat at the Battle of Badr and were now looking for revenge at Uhud. Once again, Ali was on center stage. He fought so valiantly that it was impossible for anyone to confront him. The battle began just as it did at Badr; however, a brief moment of negligence and failing to comprehend the importance of obedience led to a disaster. Muslims were about to declare victory when suddenly things took a drastic turn. The fate of the battle was about to change and lives were in grave danger. In order to break through, gallant lions like Ali were needed.

Let us listen to Ali's explanation of the dramatic events that occurred at a juncture where chaos had taken over the Battle of Uhud: "At one stage during the battle, I could not see God's Messenger. He was not amongst the martyrs either. Then I thought to myself, 'By God, the noble Messenger would never flee from the battle field. The only other possibility is that God's wrath came down upon us due to our mistakes, and He has taken him away from us. From this point on, I have no other option but to fight till death.' Then I smashed the sheath of my sword and charged towards the enemy lines. As I broke through the enemy lines, I saw the noble Messenger in combat."[24]

---

[24] Ibn Abi Ya'la, *Musnad*, 1/415 (546).

On the one hand, Ali fought relentlessly to fulfill his obligation; on the other, he tried to protect the Messenger of God, peace and blessings be upon him. The banner of Islam had fallen to the ground from the hands of Mus'ab, who had been pruned like a tree.[25] He had shown tremendous exertion to keep the banner upright using his chest. Sadly, a spear pierced through his young body, and Mus'ab fell to the ground and became a martyr of Uhud. The noble Messenger instructed Ali to pick up the banner. Ali grabbed the banner and reorganized the Muslim lines. Soon after, the noble Prophet complimented Ali with the following statement: "There is no youth like Ali, no sword like (his sword) Zulfiqar!"[26]

During the battle Ali had received a number of serious injuries that no one could cure. Sixteen of the injuries could have been fatal. He had fallen to the ground several times, but courageously he stood up each time and continued to fight. Finally, the noble Messenger was informed

---

[25] At the Battle of Uhud, the Prophet appointed Mus'ab ibn Umayr to carry the Muslim standard. The Muslims' early success in the battle was reversed when a group of Muslims, against the Prophet's orders, deserted their positions. The polytheist Quraysh forces rallied and counterattacked. Their main target, as they cut through the Muslim forces, was the noble Prophet. Mus'ab realized this danger. He raised the standard high in one hand and his sword in the other and plunged into the Quraysh forces. A Quraysh horseman moved in close and severed his right hand. He held the standard between the stumps of his arms against his chest when his left hand was also severed.

[26] Ibn Hisham, *as-Siratu'n-Nabawiyya*, 4/51.

of Ali's injuries, he said: "A man who endures such suffering for the sake of God can be excused for anything."

The temporary chaos experienced at Uhud was costly. The noble Messenger had a gash on his face and two of his sanctified teeth had been broken. Against all odds, first aid had to be applied to the noble Prophet, peace and blessings be upon him, even if it meant the removal of his noble tooth. A short while later, Fatima and Ali applied medical treatment to the noble Messenger, wiping the blood off his face.[27]

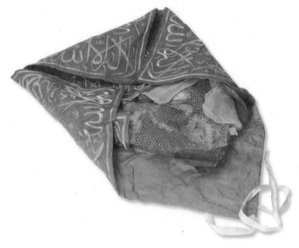

The Bridal Veil of Fatima az-Zahra
Topkapi Palace Museum, Inventory no. 21/480

---

[27] *Sahih al-Bukhari*, 3/1066 (2754).

FORMING A NEW BOND

Two years had gone by since the Migration to Medina and the noble Messenger was in the process of preparing the grounds to wed his beloved daughter Fatima to Ali, his brother in faith, proximate supporter, and the precious pupil of his eye.

One of the Companions of the noble Prophet had heard that another Companion was intending to ask for the hand of the noble Messenger's daughter. Quickly, he came to Ali and encouraged him to ask for the hand of Fatima, suggesting that he deserved her more than anyone.

However, Ali did not have the sufficient funds or wealth to marry the Prophet's beloved daughter. "How could I marry her when I have nothing?" he argued.

The wise Companion who could predict the outcome insisted: "Just go…he will let you marry her."

Who would not wish to be related to the Messenger of God? Could anyone turn down the opportunity to take someone like Fatima as a spouse, especially when she resembled her father with all her manners such as sitting, speaking, and walking?

Ali blushed with timidity as he could not refuse the persistent advice of the Companion anymore. He decided to visit the Prophet, peace and blessings be upon him. As he came face to face with the majestic figure of the Prophet, he felt quite bashful. It was as if Ali had swallowed his tongue. The Sultan of words took control of the situation, as he sensed something in Ali's voice: "Why are you here...do you need something?" he asked.

Ali was in no position to utilize this golden opportunity given to him. Once again, he bowed his head timidly. Ali preferred to keep silent as the noble Messenger realized that he had to be more open. With a soft tone of voice, he said, "I have a feeling that you came to ask for Fatima's hand in marriage."

Ali felt so humiliated that he could not say anything. Nevertheless, he wanted to marry Fatima, and he could not just stand there without replying to a question asked by the Prophet. In humility, he raised his head a fraction and softly said, "Yes..."

The noble Prophet did not wish to humiliate Ali anymore as he asked: "Do you have anything to give as *mahr*?"[28]

Could anyone attain such happiness in life? It was obvious that the noble Messenger had given consent to this marriage. Unfortunately, Ali had nothing to offer, so he replied: "No."

And it was the whole truth. He had never made the effort to accumulate worldly wealth. He had one objective

---

[28] *Mahr*, a mandatory condition of marriage in Islam, is a sum of money or property to be paid to the bride. Unlike a dowry, which a bride brings to the marriage, *mahr* is given by the groom to the bride.

in life, and that was to carry the message of the noble Messenger to every soul. He had dedicated his life to the mission of the person who was closer to him than a father. The noble Messenger was also aware of Ali's financial situation, but it was a religious principle to offer something to the bride. The solution would also come from the noble Messenger as he asked: "What have you done with the armor I had given you?"

Obviously, Ali had the armor in his possession. Without doubt, the noble Messenger wanted this marriage to take place, and he would conduct the ceremony himself. This marriage contract would establish the foundations of a house that continued his noble generation.[29]

We should pay attention and listen carefully to what is about to occur here. The last Messenger of God, who had been complimented with the title "Habibullah" by the Almighty Himself, was giving his beloved daughter Fatima's hand in marriage for an armor received as *mahr*.

This was a partnership that lasted for eight years until Fatima's death. After Khadija, Fatima was the most blessed woman on earth. One may even say that this was a marriage performed by the hands of the noble Messenger and sanctified by the heavens and beyond. This blessed marriage produced three boys named Hasan, Husayn, and Muhsin (who died during birth), and two girls by the name of Zaynab and Umm Kulthum.

---

[29] Ibn Hanbal, *Musnad*, 1/80 (603).

The Messenger of God, Ali, and Fatima… Three people who had dedicated their lives to God. It is not hard to predict the family life of these three exemplary individuals. This family would be a role-model for all believers.

They lived in the same conditions as most of the Prophet's Companions. They endured hardship in unity. The beloved daughter of the Prophet spun the mill with her own hands until she had blisters all over them. She took on all house duties and performed them by herself. Ali was deeply concerned about her as she struggled with daily chores, but he was in no different situation himself. Ali also worked hard to earn their living; he picked dates and drew water out of the well. Often, he would come home with cuts and sores all over his hands.

One day, Ali heard that prisoners of war were brought to Medina. He went to the noble Messenger and requested a servant to help Fatima at home. The noble Messenger was not pleased with Ali's request because those in the leading group were supposed to be leaders also in enduring hardship and difficulties. They had to abstain from surrendering to the attractive comforts of this transient world. That meant living a difficult life but a peaceful one through the remembrance of God, and no doubt this was more blessed than asking for a servant. Therefore, the noble Messenger suggested: "As you enter your bed, recite 'Subhanallah' thirty-three times, 'Alhamdulillah' thirty-three times, and 'Allahu Akbar' thirty-four times. This is more blessed for you than a servant."[30]

---

[30] *Sahih al-Bukhari*, 3/1133 (2945).

A MAN OF IMPERATIVE DUTIES

Excluding the expedition to Tabuk (**630** CE), Ali participated in all battles. During the battle of Tabuk he was asked to remain in Medina as a representative of the Prophet. Ali never disobeyed an order in his entire life; however, he could not bring himself to accept such a duty. Quickly, he left Medina and caught up with the Prophet. Upon seeing the Prophet, he said: "Are you leaving me behind with women and children?"

He was dismayed by the whole thing because Ali was a man of the front lines. He was extremely disappointed about being left out of the battle field where the spirit of munificence peaked, where lives and wealth were risked. The noble Messenger consoled Ali and explained how important he was to him: "Oh Ali, would you not wish to be with me in the status that Aaron was next to Moses? There would be only one difference, and that is no Prophet will come after me."[31]

Ali, may God be pleased with him, became the sought after man of special and practical duties. He had written the conditions of the famous Treaty of Hudaybiyah. He was given the duty of informing Abu Bakr—who was

---

[31] *Sahih Muslim*, 4/1870 (2404).

leading the pilgrims to Mecca for the Hajj—of the most recent revelations and rulings. There were times when he was the scribe of the Divine Revelations, and when necessary, he fought like a gallant lion on the battle fields.

On the day of Hudaybiyah, when it was time to write down the conditions of the treaty, the noble Messenger summoned Ali and said: "Write, 'In the Name of Allah, the All-Merciful and the All-Compassionate.'"

The noble Messenger had not even completed his sentence when Suhayl ibn Amr, the official envoy of the Quraysh, intervened with a protest. He argued against the words, "All-Merciful" and "All-Compassionate", claiming that if they had faith in these words there would be no conflict between the two parties in the first place. He insisted that the words be removed from the agreement. The noble Messenger was a man of peace and did not wish put things in jeopardy because of Suhayl's obsession with two words. Thus, he agreed to the removal of the words. Once again he asked Ali to write: "This is a treaty made between Muhammad the Messenger of Allah and Suhayl ibn Amr."

Once more, Suhayl intervened: "Do not write 'Muhammad the Messenger of God!' If we had accepted your Prophethood, we would not have gone into battle with you."

He was suggesting that the Prophet's name should be written as Muhammad the son of Abdullah. The noble Messenger turned to Ali and said: "Rub it out!"

He was asking Ali to remove the words "Messenger of Allah." What difference was it going to make? Nevertheless, Ali could not bring himself to do this. He glanced at the Prophet with an expression that meant, "Isn't this a bit too much?" The Prophet's eyes conveyed the message "For the sake of peace and harmony, I would agree to the removal of my name." The noble Messenger was determined.[32] But how could this be? He was asking Ali to rub out the words "Messenger of God" from the agreement. Ali thought about it for a brief moment and said, "I cannot rub this out, Oh Messenger of Allah!"

How could he take these words out? These were the words they had tried to convey at every opportunity they found.

Seeing Ali's sensitivity on the issue, the noble Messenger took it upon himself to change the words from "The Messenger of God" to "Muhammad the son of Abdullah."[33]

Since he was five years old, Ali had never left the side of the Prophet, excluding a few occasions when the noble Messenger himself had assigned him to certain duties. His knowledge of the Qur'an was so vast that in a mere six months, he arranged the verses in the sequence in which they were revealed. To get some understanding of his knowledge about the Qur'an, we need to take a look at the

---

[32] In the Treaty of Hudaybiyah, which took place between the state of Medina and the Quraysh tribe of Mecca in 628 CE, the two sides agreed to stop fighting for a period of ten years. The aftermath of the talks shows all the efforts of the Prophet for a peaceful settlement coming to success as Islam began to spread widely and quickly after the signing of the treaty.

[33] *Sahih Muslim*, 3/1409; Sallabi, *Ali ibn Abi Talib*, 116.

noble Messenger's statement regarding Ali: "If I am the city of knowledge, Ali is the gate of this city. Whoever needs to obtain knowledge should enter through this gate."[34]

Ali always carried a page in the sheath of his sword on which he had written out some Hadith during the time of the Prophet, peace and blessings be upon him. The page contained information and rulings regarding matters such as the amount of compensation to be paid in cases of death or wounding; the strategies to be used in saving Muslim prisoners from the hands of the enemy; a rule stating that a Muslim could not be killed to save the life of a nonbeliever; and information about the boundaries of the state of Medina and the inviolate sacred zone of the Haram.[35]

He was so sensitive when it came to Hadith narrations that he would make the person who transmitted the Hadith take an oath stating that he had heard the Hadith from the noble Prophet himself.

A person who had achieved profundity in faith had to refrain from the world or the world had to abandon him. Ali had achieved the deepest profundity in faith, and he was continuously tested with the most difficult tragedies and heartbreaks in life. His beloved mother Fatima had also passed away, and besides the noble Prophet, there was no one left to support him.

When Ali's mother, Fatima passed away, the noble Messenger sent his own cloak to be used as a shroud, and

---

[34] Hakim, *Mustadrak*, 3/137 (4637).
[35] *Sahih al-Bukhari*, 6/2662 (6870).

during the burial he placed the body into the grave with his own hands. The noble Messenger knew very well the feeling of losing one's mother. When asked why he took so much interest in this funeral, he said: "After my mother passed away, Fatima was like a mother to me. I will never forget the compassion and empathy she had shown towards me."[36] The Prophet had displayed the importance of fidelity with an expression that reflected his admiration for Fatima.

The noble Messenger would visit his daughter and son-in-law from time to time asking how they were. One day he visited them and realized that Ali was not home. He asked Fatima for the whereabouts of her husband. As it happened with all families, they had had a small misunderstanding between them, and Ali had left the house deciding that he needed some time to solve the issue. The noble Messenger could not bear to see his son-in-law in a miserable state. He had raised Ali in his own house. The problem had to be solved as soon as possible because great marriages in which the delicate winds of tranquility and love blew all over the house should not be put in jeopardy with such insignificant issues. He stood up and went out to look for Ali. Where could a hero of faith, whose nights were as bright as his days, have gone? As the Prophet had predicted, Ali was at the Masjid. He had fallen asleep from exhaustion. The noble Messenger approached him and touched Ali with the tip of his noble foot. Then

---

[36] Hakim, *Mustadrak*, 3/116 (4573).

staring at him compassionately, with a soft tone of voice, he said: "Wake up, Oh Abu Turab!"

This was a delicate jest, as Abu Turab meant, "The father of the earth." Ali had placed his head on the ground as he slept, and there were marks left on his face. As he stood up, he had dust rolling off his face. The noble Messenger's compliment gave Ali a sense of delight. He enjoyed the title "the father of the earth."

Fatima az-Zahra's prayer rug which was embroidered at a later date
Topkapi Palace Museum, Inventory no. 21/14

THE MEMBERS OF THE NOBLE
MESSENGER'S HOUSEHOLD

I t was a great honor that whenever the term "House-hold of the Messenger of God" was mentioned, Ali came to mind. One day, the noble Messenger placed his cloak on Fatima, Ali, Hasan and Husayn, and then recited the following verse:

> God only wills to remove from you, O members of the (Prophet's) Household, all that may be loath-some and to purify you to the utmost of purity. (Ahzab 33:33)

In another incident, the noble Messenger had invited the Christians of Najran to embrace Islam.[37] A delegation from

---

[37] Indeed, God's Messenger had been sending official letters to different countries and their rulers, inviting them to Islam. Among these were two different invitations that had been sent to the Christians of Najran. In receipt of the letters, a delegation from the Christians of Najran decided to visit the Prophet. When the Najran delegation that was made up of about sixty well-educated Christians reached Medina, they debated with the Prophet in an investigatory dialogue for two days in the Mosque of the Prophet. God's Messenger provided them with a place close to his mosque to stay and allowed them to say their prayers in the mosque. Though the delegation had disagreements with the Prophet at the meetings about the nature of Jesus, peace be upon him, and the

the Christians of Najran decided to visit the Prophet in 631 CE. Due to disagreements during the exchanges of dialogue, they agreed to have a *mubahala* (which means invoking God's curse on the party that lies as a means to prove one's truthfulness), taking place in the open the next day. The Prophet emerged out of his house the following day, taking Ali, Fatima, Hasan, and Husayn along to the organized meeting. He said: "Oh God, this is my family!" and continued with the following verses from the holy Qur'an:

> (The creation of) Jesus in reference to God resembles (the creation of) Adam. He created him from earth, then said He to him, "Be!" and he is. (As the truth always consists in what your Lord wills and decrees,) so is this the truth from your Lord (in this matter); do not then be, (and you are never expected to be,) of those who doubt. After the (true) knowledge has come to you, whoever still disputes with you about him (Jesus), say (in challenging them): "Come, then! Let us summon our sons and your sons, and our women and your women, our selves and your selves, and then let us pray and invoke God's curse upon those who lie." (Al Imran 3:59–61)

The Prophet suggested that if they were genuinely sincere in their cause then they would risk their own lives for it through a mutual cursing. However, when the

---

concept of the Divine Being, who does not beget, nor is He begotten, and none is comparable unto Him, they agreed to make a social pact with him and returned to Najran with a written assurance provided by the Prophet that their lives, property, and religion would be protected.

Christians of Najran saw the Prophet with Husayn sitting on his lap, Hasan holding his hand, and Ali and Fatima standing by him, they changed their minds. They realized how determined the noble Messenger was when they heard him say to his Household: "When I pray you should say Amin!"[38]

The fact of the matter was that this was no issue to be taken lightly. Avoiding calling on God to inflict His wrath on them if they lied, the delegation backed out of taking an oath that they were right and true in their claims and agreed to enter into a treaty with the Prophet and to live under Muslim rule.

This *mubahala* incident clearly shows how close Ali was to the Prophet as a member of his Household, called the *Ahlu'l-Bayt*. Of course, Ali's proximity to the noble Messenger of God was not limited by this example. One day the noble Messenger would pull him aside and say: "You are of me and I of you."[39] This was a sign of unity, loyalty, and a meeting of *Habib* (the Beloved) and *Mahbub* (the Loved) on the same path.

---

[38] Qurtubi, *Tafsiru'l-Qurtubi*, 4/104.
[39] *Sahih al-Bukhari*, 2/960 (2552).

THE BANNER BEARER
OF THE HEROES

Ali, may God be pleased with him, was a man of solution. When it was necessary, he would solve problems with ease. Conversely, when he was needed on the battle field, he would roar like a lion, sending shivers down the spines of his enemies. In most cases, problems would be solved upon the mentioning of his name.

The Sakif tribe caused conflicts with their instigations. The Messenger of God sent them a warning: "Abstain from this attitude at once or I shall send you a man who will remove your heads, make prisoners of your families, and collect your wealth as spoils of war."

The man he was referring to in his message was no other than Ali. The reply was a quick one. There was no need for Ali to go there anymore because they decided to solve their own problems.[40]

In another incident, Khaybar was laid siege since they had allied with the tribes of Quraysh and Banu Ghatafan to attack Medina, but the strong fortress of Khaybar

---

40 Ibn Abdil Barr, *Istiab*, 3/1110.

would not fall. Nevertheless, it was a place that had to be conquered due to their continual treachery. The time had arrived, and the noble Messenger said, "Tomorrow I will place the banner in the hands of such a person that by his hands God will grant victory, for he loves God and His Messenger and is loved by them."

Was there an honor and rank higher than this? This choice earned Ali the title of "al-Murtada" (the one with whom God is pleased). It was a day on which even Companions such as Umar, who had always abstained from the desire to be the leader, said: "By Allah, never in my life had I wished so much to be the leader on that day. I always hoped that the noble Messenger would point at me and say, 'He is the one.'"

It was a night that no one could sleep. Everyone wished that they would be the one who was loved by God and His Messenger. They all imagined themselves as the bearer of the banner. Finally, the awaited time had arrived with the break of dawn. The noble Messenger's eyes were searching for someone. It was quite obvious that the person sought after was not amongst them. He asked, "Where is Ali?"

Quickly, they informed Ali, and he rushed to appear before the Prophet, peace and blessings be upon him. Everyone waited anxiously, wondering what the noble Messenger would say. Finally, he spoke: "Here is the man I am looking for!"

That day Ali had an infection in his eyes. God's Messenger applied his sanctified saliva on them and prayed for

Ali. The noble Prophet then handed the banner over to
Ali. Chronic eye infections had dragged this valiant hero
into bed. However, from that day on, he would never suffer from such an illness again. There was no sign of hesitation on Ali's face as he grabbed the banner and strode
out. How could one hesitate or turn back from a mission
assigned by the noble Messenger? As Ali walked away, he
asked without turning his head around: "Will I fight until
they become Muslims like us?"

The answer suggested that the first aim would be to
invite them to Islam, and even if it was necessary to fight,
the notion of calling them into submission to God should
never be forgotten. The noble Messenger explained this
with the following statement:

> By God, if one of them embraces the faith by the will
> of God and through your hands, this is more blessed
> than being the owner of a valley full of red camels[41]
> and donating them for the sake of God.[42]

Then the battle of Khaybar commenced. There were
many legends about Khaybar, and one of them was a man
called Mahrab. The chieftains of Khaybar encouraged him
to confront Ali. However, no one was a challenge to Ali
anymore. Hence, he finished Mahrab off with a single

---

[41] Red camels were very precious in Arab society at the time. A person
who owned such a camel was considered rich, and extremely few
people owned an entire herd of red camels. This analogy, therefore,
clearly shows the value of guiding a single person to the right path.

[42] *Sahih Muslim*, 4/1872 (2406).

move. Upon seeing this, the noble Messenger became jovial as he said: "Be merry, because Khaybar will soon fall."

There was great confusion on that day. At one stage, Ali had dropped his shield, and there was nothing to protect him from the constant attacks. Everyone was in panic wondering what Ali would do next. As Ali glanced around, he saw the gates of the fortress lying on the ground. It was obvious that he had a plan. Quickly he bent over and grabbed the gate by its handle. Then he roared like a lion, shouting the words, "Allahu Akbar!" What kind of a concentration was this? Ali had tapped into a mysterious metaphysical force to pick up a colossal gate in order to use it as a shield.

With the gate in his hand, Ali broke through a large group of men, opening gaps within the enemy lines.

Abu Rafi, the beloved Companion of the Prophet said, "After the incident, along with seven of my friends we attempted to lift the gate off the ground. By God, we could not even move it."[43]

Nevertheless, Ali's good manners, humility, and modesty never changed, even on the battle fields. During the battle of Badr, with one blow he had dropped Abu Sa'd ibn Abi Talha to the ground. Ali was about to make his final move to finish him off when he suddenly backed away. A few of Ali's friends approached him and asked why he had done this. Ali replied: "I was about to finish

---

[43] Ibn Kathir, *al-Bidaya wa'n-Nihaya*, 4/189.

him off when I saw that his private parts were exposed. To avoid staring at *haram*, I moved away from him."[44]

---

44 Tabari, *Tarikhu'l-Umam wa'l-Muluk*, 2/63.

MAN OF THE NIGHT

Ali had sustained many injuries during the battles he participated in along the side of the noble Messenger of God. Protecting the Prophet was a priority for Ali, so without any hesitation he would risk his life in order to defend him. This gallant lion fought vigorously on the battle fields, but he was also a spiritual man of the night.

As the darkness of the night blanketed his evenings, he would go to prostration and worship his Lord. His submission and prayers contained so much depth that when he went to prostration, you could hear a noise which sounded like a volcano had erupted in him. Whenever his dear friend Bilal, who was also a refugee from Mecca, began to call the Adhan, Ali would begin to tremble like a person who had malaria and his face would turn pale.

He performed all duties entrusted to him with perfection. He would never use an excuse to withdraw from a mission. Swinging his sword through the battle fields during the day when it was necessary was not an obstacle to his bright sanctified nights. He knew that his path was to take the name of his Lord to the four corners of the world, and in order to achieve this goal, his nights had to be as bright as his days.

One day, the believers asked our mother, Aisha: "Which woman does the noble Messenger of Allah loves the most?" Without hesitation, she replied, "Fatima." Then they asked, "How about amongst the men?" "Fatima's husband," she replied.

According to Aisha, the reason that the noble Prophet loved Ali so much was this: "To my knowledge, he would spend his nights praying and his days fasting."[45]

Everyone had acknowledged the fact that after the Prophet, Ali would be the spiritual scholar of Muslims. This was a good tiding announced publicly by the Prophet himself. As Ibn Abbas stated, when the Qur'an says, "Oh you who believe," Ali must be the initial person addressed.[46]

Following the battle of Tabuk, the Messenger of God decided to send Ali to Yemen. There, he invited people to embrace the religion of God and His Messenger. Upon hearing the news, Ali came to the noble Messenger and said, "Oh Messenger of God...You are sending me to Yemen, where the people will ask me about rulings of Islam. I do not possess the sufficient knowledge for this mission." The noble Messenger said, "Approach!"

Ali came closer to the Prophet. Then the noble Prophet tapped Ali softly on the chest and prayed, "Oh Allah! Grant Ali the power of speech and bless him with a righteous heart."

---

[45] Hakim, *Mustadrak*, 3/171 (4744).
[46] Haythami, *Majmau'z-Zawaid*, 9/125.

Sometime later, Ali stated, "By the One who creates the seed out of the atom, from that day on, I have never hesitated in making a judgment regarding any conflict between two people."[47]

Ali, the sought after man of the battle fields, was so modest in his daily life that his manners and behavior was admired by everyone. His munificence and power of representation had won the hearts of many people. In no time, they were coming tribe after tribe to embrace Islam.

When the Muslims conquered Mecca, the city they had to leave as refugees, the noble Messenger once again gave Ali the duty of destroying the idols in the Ka'ba. As Ali began to destroy the idols, he recited the verses that announced the arrival of the Truth and the downfall of falsehood. He also worked briskly to prepare the Ka'ba for praying the Salah before the noble had Messenger arrived.

The farewell Hajj was the first and only Hajj performed by the Messenger of God. It was during the Hajj that he bid farewell to his followers (*ummah*). At the time, Ali was not in Mecca. The noble Messenger had sent him to Yemen to invite the people of Yemen to Islam. One by one, Ali visited people in their homes to convey the message. His only desire was to plant the love of God in their hearts. As soon as he heard about the Prophet's farewell Hajj, he left Yemen for Mecca. How could Ali be absent from a place where the noble Prophet would address his

---

[47] Ibn Abi Shayba, *Musannaf*, 6/365 (32068).

community for the last time? Quickly, he came to Mecca to join thousands of people who stood before the Prophet at Arafat as he delivered his Farewell Sermon.

There was no doubt about Ali's power of judgment and sagacity. One day, a man came to him asking about destiny. He said, "It is an immense ocean, and once you dive in it, you will not come out again." However, the man continued to insist. Ali added, "It is a mystery that belongs to God; you cannot comprehend. Therefore, do not delve into it so much."

Conversely, the man was relentless as he constantly insisted on receiving some kind of explanation. Ali, may God be pleased with him, asked, "Oh you, who asks this question! Did God create you the way He wished or the way you wanted?" "He created me the way He willed!" replied the man. Then Ali concluded, "The power of disposal is in His grasp, and He decrees as He wills."[48]

---

[48] Haythami, *as-Sawaiqu'l-Muhriqa*, 2/382; Mubarakfuri, *Tuhfatu'l-Ahwadhi*, 6/279.

THE SORROW OF THE
PARTING DAY

A day would come when even the Eternal Light would eventually set. He was also a human being and like all mortals, he would set sail towards "The Exalted Friend" upon the completion of his mission. Unfortunately, that day had arrived. The highest peak had been conquered, and there was no higher level to attain on earth. So the time to migrate to the eternal world called *uqba* had come for the noble Prophet, peace and blessings be upon him.

Ali melted down like a candle wax upon the setting of the Eternal Sun. Losing someone who had been the most valuable entity in his life from the first day he had cast eyes on him was an unbearable sorrow that engulfed Ali's horizon. He was in shock…had he not possessed a steel-hard faith, he would have chosen to go with him. However, many important duties awaited him. Ali was being prepared in a unique way for the ever more difficult days that lay ahead.

There was also the will of the master of masters. When the time had come for the Prophet to open his wings to fly towards the eternal world, Ali would take on the duty of making the funeral arrangements.

According to worldly standards, the source of life that gave life to the universe was not breathing anymore. A heart that gave life to many hearts was not beating anymore. He had worn out his own body in order to resurrect the lifeless hearts of others. As his noble eyes turned towards eternity, even his lifeless body was emitting a lucid message to those who understood. The light that was born in Mecca should not have been limited to the Arabian Peninsula. It had to be taken to four corners of the world.

Washing his noble body must have been quite painful for Ali, may God be pleased with him. It was as if he was washing him with tears that flowed like fountains. The duty of wrapping him in a winding-sheet and placing his noble body into the grave was also given to Ali. At one stage, Ali's wife Fatima, the daughter of the noble Prophet, had lost control and was screaming out to those who were about to lay to rest the noble body of the Prophet, "How could you be willing to throw soil on the Messenger of Allah!"

Once again, it was Ali who consoled her. In the days ahead, the two of them would stare at each other, only to burst into tears as they remembered the days they had spent with Prophet Muhammad, peace and blessings be upon him. Everything reminded them of him...

They had found their identity through the teachings of the noble Messenger, and they had nourished their souls with the knowledge of Islam to become the living embodiment of the Qur'an. They had obtained the structure to continue the rest of the way on their own. God's Messenger was no longer with them. However, the sanctified values that they had obtained from him were enough to brighten their lives and to solve all problems that may have emerged for the rest of their lives.

One of the earliest photographs of the Qubbat al-Khadra (Green Dome) over the Prophet's tomb constructed by Sultan Mahmud II (circa 1880s)

GENEROSITY AND MODESTY

He was so munificent that even on days when he was suffering from starvation he would give the little food he had to others who needed it more. According to Ali, the world had less value than the wings of a fly. Once, he had clearly stated, "I have divorced the world through three *talaqs*[49] with a vow never to turn back."[50]

One day he had a vision in which the world had appeared before him. He said: "Oh world! Disappear from my sight! Oh world! You cannot deceive me, go find someone else!"[51]

According to Ali, the world was a place from which both the good and the bad benefitted. However, the Judgment Day was inevitable, and it was a day on which only the Power of the true Possessor would prevail. The thing he feared the most in life was losing himself in worldly affairs by following the enticements of the carnal soul and consequently failing to remember death.[52]

As the noble Messenger had suggested, Ali closed all doors leading to worldly temptations and dedicated his

---

[49] The term "three *talaqs*" is an irreversible decree used for divorcing in an irreconcilable manner.

[50] Abu Nuaym, *Hilyatu'l-Awliya*, 1/85.

[51] Ibid.

[52] al-Bayhaqi, *Shuabu'l-Iman*, 7/369 (10614).

life to the path of Allah. When he returned to Mecca during his mission in Yemen to join the farewell Hajj of the noble Prophet, Ali appointed a person to represent him as a leader to the group of men under his supervision. As a gesture, Ali's representative bought new clothes for the men he was in charge of so that they appeared presentable before the noble Prophet. Upon seeing this, Ali shouted with resentment: "Shame on you! Change these clothes before we reach the noble Messenger!"

The order was obeyed, but it caused a disturbance amongst the soldiers. They felt as if they had been insulted. When they appeared before the Prophet, they complained about the changes made by Ali. No doubt, this was anticipated behavior on Ali's behalf. The noble Messenger addressed the soldiers on the matter and said: "Oh people! Do not complain about Ali. He has strict principles when it comes to serving God, so do not complain!"[53]

Ali's personality never changed; he was the same person that day as he was the day before. Time did not change him, and it would never be able to do so..! The concept of *taqwa* (God consciousness and piety) had taken control of his world; therefore, in his interactions with people, he did not act upon his emotions but upon the values prescribed by God and His Messenger. This attitude did not even change during the battles. On the day of Siffin when Muawiya and his men had targeted and questioned Ali's authority as Caliph, Ibn Abbas said to him,

---

[53] Ibn Hanbal, *Musnad*, 3/86 (11865).

"War is stratagem...Use stratagem to overwhelm them!"
Ali replied: "By God, no! I would never change my religion for their world!"[54]

Even on the days when he distributed thousands of
Dinars as charity, he would wrap stones around his waist
to control his hunger. He always thought of others.[55]
There were days when he suffered from starvation, yet he
continued to work, carrying water from the wells and
picking dates to earn enough money to buy something to
eat. Then he would quickly come next to the Prophet.[56]
He lived a simple life. Most of the time, he would lie
down on the sand and wear clothes that were covered with
patches. His garments were made of rough fabrics. When
asked why he chose to dress that way, he said, "This is
more serene." He also argued that those who had no other option but to wear such clothes would feel better seeing him that way.[57]

One day, some suggested that his clothes were not suitable for the status of the Caliphate. They said that he
should be wearing garments made from quality materials.
This was a proposal he firmly contested. According to Ali,
a Caliph did not rule with his clothes. He ruled with the
sensitivity and responsibility he felt towards Allah. Appear-
ing as he had broken all bonds with God was not a right
thing to do. Before long, Ali answered those around him:

---

[54] Tabari, *Tarikhu'l-Umam wa'l-Muluk*, 2/704.

[55] Ibn Hanbal, *Musnad*, 1/159 (1367).

[56] al-Hannad, *Zuhd*, 2/385 (749).

[57] Ibid., 2/368 (705).

"These clothes protect me from arrogance and haughtiness. At the same time, they enhance the sense of tranquility during the daily prayers."[58]

Some days he sold his sword at the grand bazaar of Kufa in order to purchase a piece of clothing material. Ali was the leader of Muslims and a Caliph of the Messenger of God during these days. If he had wished, the wealth of the world would have been at his disposal, and no one would have criticized him.

However, he knew that the noble Messenger and the Prophets before him carried poverty on their shoulders like an ornament and without any hesitation. On the day that the great guide, the master of masters, peace and blessings be upon him, had passed away, his shield was at the hands of a Jew who had kept it as collateral. With the wisdom Ali received from the Qur'an, he knew that Prophet Moses, peace be upon him, beseeched poverty from his Lord as if it was a valuable treasure. According to him, anything granted in this regard was to be considered as great wealth. Prophet Jesus, peace be upon him, also chose to live a life of poverty; he preferred wearing ragged clothes over the temptations of the world. This is why most of the time Ali's mount was his feet and his servants were his hands. Instead of being indebt to others, he preferred to do his own chores. When asked why, he replied:

> Refusing to share the burdens of life with others
> while they acknowledge me as the Ruler of the Faith-

---

58 Ibnu'l-Mubarak, *Zuhd*, 1/261 (756).

ful feels quite unfair to me. By God, if I wish, I could obtain the purest honey, quality wheat, and the most expensive clothes. However, I fear that I would be overwhelmed by the temptations of my carnal soul and ego. As a result, I will fail to notice those who suffer from starvation and poverty.

Ali not only lived a modest life, he also advised those under his command to do the same. He wanted his viziers and governors to live a life similar to poorest people. He would say to those who criticized him, "If this wealth had belonged to me, I would have distributed it equally amongst the people. However, this wealth belongs to God, and these are the servants of God."[59]

He was referring to the wealth possessed by the treasury department. He wanted that wealth to reach the poor and the needy, not those who were in authority. "Allah has granted wealth to the rich so that the poor could benefit. If the wealthy had performed their duty in a righteous manner, poverty and famine would diminish," he frequently said.[60]

One day, his men came to Ali and informed him that the treasury had accumulated an abundance of wealth. Upon hearing this, he recited *takbir*. Then quickly he went to the treasury department and made the following statement, "Oh gold coins! Oh shining silver! You cannot deceive me…Go knock on another door!"

---

[59]   Ibn Abdil Barr, *Istiab*, 3/1111.
[60]   al-Bayhaqi, *as-Sunanu'l-Kubra*, 7/23 (12985).

Then he made a gesture with his hand, indicating that everything had to be distributed. Before long, there was not a single gold or silver coin left in the treasury.

Then he ordered a thorough cleaning of the place. Quickly, he praised God by uttering "Allahu Akbar" and performed two *rakat*s (units) of prayer there. He believed that two *rakat*s performed here would testify on his behalf on the Day of Judgment.[61]

Following his death, Dirar ibn Damrah mourned for him with poetry. In an elegy Dirar wrote:

> I remember him saying one day, "Oh world! Oh World! I know you have beautified yourself with decorations and wait impatiently to come to me. Do not waste your time; you will only tire yourself out. Go pick on someone else if you have the strength! I have divorced you through three *talaq*s, never to return on my word. You have a short lifespan and your living standards are low; however, the detriment you cause is enormous. Shame on you! The journey is long, and there are many obstacles, yet rations are scarce!"[62]

Upon hearing this, Muawiya walked up to him and said: "May God have mercy on Hasan's father. He was exactly as you described." Then he continued with a question, "You felt so much pain following Ali's death. What was the magnitude of your sorrow?" Dirar replied, "I felt the pain of a mother carrying her strangled child!"[63]

---

[61] Sallabi, *Ali ibn Abi Talib*, 245–246.
[62] Abu Nuaym, *Hilyatu'l-Awliya*, 1/85.
[63] Ibid.

As he was the leader in piety and righteousness, he was also a leader in generosity and munificence. One day, he led the Morning Prayer and was sitting with his companions. He looked quite innocent and worried. The companions became concerned with his appearance, so they formed a circle around him. Out of respect, no one asked him anything. They just wished to share his sadness. Then the rays of the rising sun brightened the mosque's interior. Ali recuperated and stood up to perform two *rakat*s of prayer. His face had turned pale as he shook his head with heartache. Then he began to speak:

> By God, I have seen the Companions of the Prophet. Alas, I cannot find anyone like them today. Without question, when they reached the morning, you would see the brilliance of the night upon their faces. They would spend their nights in prostration and recite the Qur'an. They would pray all night, sometimes standing, sometimes in the lying position. When they remembered God, they would shake like a tree and weep until their clothes soaked with tears.[64]

As Ali emphasized in his famous sermon, an ideal believer had to possess the two unique qualities: knowledge and the skill of spiritual contemplation. Moreover, a believer had to abstain from the temptations of the world. The inevitable life of eternity (*akhirah*) was the true realm of all human beings. As the sons of the earth wasted their lives running after the transient world, those who had their eyes fixed on eternity used this world as a stepping stone to

---

[64] Abu'l-Faraj, *Sifatu's-Safwah*, 1/331.

obtain a life of eternal happiness. This was the only way, and to prove it one had to refrain from the bodily temptations and use his energy to seek the pleasure of God. Indeed, life on earth was very short, and in order to earn the eternal happiness, one had to travel this short distance with great patience. In this regard, to achieve success, one had to live as those before him, brightening the nights with submission and seeking the pleasure of Allah during the days. Yes, those unique Companions of the Prophet utilized their nights so perfectly that during the day, their faces looked so pale that people assumed they were ill even though they were not ill, nor did they abstain from living a normal life. There was an important nuance here, and it was more significant than anything presumed.

Ali was also extremely modest. He would always do his own shopping and business dealings at the market. He would never allow others to carry his bags for him; even those who insisted relentlessly were not permitted to do so.[65] When he entered a shop with his servant, he would wait until the servant chose a garment for himself, and then Ali would choose his from the leftovers.[66] He would make donations throughout the day and night, in secret and in the open. He did not wish to possess anything of value.[67] Throughout his life, he spent all his time trying to pass on the entrusted message he had received from the noble Messenger, to all those he could reach.

---

[65] Ibn Hanbal, *Fadailu's-Sahaba*, 1/546 (916).

[66] Ibid., 1/544 (911).

[67] Ibid., 1/539 (899).

They had suggested the construction of a leadership palace for him, yet he strongly declined, saying: "I will never move into a palace that has no future!"

So what do you think? Does not Ali, may God be pleased with him, continue to teach and advice us like a living scholar. Isn't it a fact that today, he continues to guide the believers with his exemplary piety and abstinence from worldly pleasures?

Indeed, he may not be amongst us physically, but this separation can only be considered a temporary heartache. Moreover, when we analyze the precious treasures he had left behind, such as piety, abstinence from worldly pleasures, fear of God, benevolence, kindness, patience, endurance, wisdom, insight, knowledge and righteous deeds, we realize that he is still in action and continues to generously distribute pearls of wisdom to those who knock on his door.

TROUBLESOME YEARS AMID
EXTREMISM AND REMISSNESS

Being so close to the Messenger of God also meant struggling with constant tests and assessments. Proximity to authority sometime meant maximum responsibility and accountability. One had to be extremely cautious in imitating the person in authority. It was also important to be alert and watchful against those who wished to take advantage of their proximity to the Prophet. The noble Messenger, who is the gentlest of people and a role model for all the self-sacrificing heroes, was always ready to put others before himself, constantly caring for them. He forgot about his own hunger, and if he had a drop of milk, he would give it to those that needed it. There were times when he gave away the garment off his back. He never expected anything in return. When he had nothing to give, he would promise help later on. He never said "no" to any request from anyone in his entire life and never turned anyone away empty handed from his door. Ali was the pupil of the seal of Prophethood; therefore, he behaved exactly as his noble master.

There was also the reality of deprivation due to proximity. Being in the service of such a great mission like Prophethood, one had to live a simple life and expect nothing from this transient world, just as the owner of the Prophethood did. Ali experienced this example first hand, thus he knew exactly what to do when certain situations arose.

Once, the Prophet's daughter Fatima had requested a servant, and it was refused. Likewise, his cousin Ibn Abbas requested leadership, and he was also turned down. Following the conquering of Mecca, Ali thought of performing certain services around the Ka'ba. He had made his intentions clear to the Prophet. The noble Messenger summoned him and said, "Without doubt, you have received your share." Then the noble Messenger gave the keys of the Ka'ba to its previous holder, Uthman ibn Talha.[68] What the Prophet meant was, "in this world, your duty is to work for the sake of Allah and act with feelings of responsibility." The Household of Muhammad was focused on giving only, and the notion of taking had been erased from their vocabulary. They gave and helped without expecting anything in return...they did not even expect a simple thank you or a compliment from anyone.

When they made their pledges to Ali as he became the Caliph, he was appointed as the ruler of one of the most powerful nations on earth. Many men would have dreamed of attaining such a position. However, Ali never thought of using this power for his own benefit. On the contrary, this power and authority had become a nightmare for Ali. If it

---

[68] Abdur Razzaq, *Musannaf*, 5/84 (9074).

had been left up to him, he would have taken this title off his shoulders and run as far as he could.

Obviously, while some would have been pleased by this, others felt quite agitated. As a result, Ali became a target for some. Indeed, everyone wanted something, and those who were not satisfied with impartiality sought other means to satisfy their carnal souls. Consequently, the heir of the noble Prophet eventually became a target of their poisonous arrows. Once the noble Prophet had indicated this when he said to Ali:

> Oh Ali! You will be like Jesus, the son of Mary. Some of the Jews were upset with him and made allegations about his mother. Whereas, some Christians raised him to a level where he could not be, this was due to their extreme love for him. They had lost their balance.[69]

Throughout his Caliphate, he struggled with these two extremes. Some loved him so much that they went to extremes by idolizing him while others accused him of blasphemy.

Even on the day of the funeral services for the noble Messenger, there were those who approached him, suggesting that he should be the next Caliph. Some even went to extremes by pledging that they would form armies to support his leadership. However, Ali pushed all of them aside with the back of his hand, saying to one of them who came to him with this proposal: "Oh Abu Hanzala! You

---

[69] al-Bayhaqi, *as-Sunanu'l-Kubra*, 5/137 (8488).

are inviting me to something that does not concur with
our nature. I have closed that door and locked it securely
so it may never to be opened again."[70]

With such strong stance, he blocked the path of those who
wished to provoke him. Before long, he made his pledge to
Abu Bakr, who was his loyal friend of the early days.

Following the Prophet's death, Ali tried hard to convince
himself that the noble Messenger was no longer with them,
but it was impossible to get use to a life without him. Wherever he turned, it was as if he was beholding his silhouette,
and his voice continuously echoed in his head. His only condolence was Fatima, the most valuable thing entrusted to Ali
by the Prophet. She was the rose of his house, yet before
long, she also joined her father, leaving Ali all alone with his
sorrows and mission. Fatima could not handle the death of
her beloved father, and she was about to go on the same
journey. Her only concern was for her children who would
be orphaned. She was looking for a solution, someone to
look after her children; therefore, she suggested to Ali that
he wed her sister Zaynab's daughter Umama after she
passed away. This was the will of Fatima.[71]

Only six months after the departure of the Prophet,
peace and blessings be upon him, from this transient world,
Fatima also joined her father and other beloved friends.
Ali's only source of condolence was no longer living.

---

[70] Tabari, *Tarikhu'l-Umam wa'l-Muluk*, 2/237.

[71] Umama was the daughter of Abu'l As, who was the son of Rabi ibn
      Adiyy and also the Prophet's son-in-law.

Although there are some reports implying that initially Ali had delayed his pledge to Abu Bakr, the reality is that he loved and respected him so much that he had named one of his sons after him. When Abu Bakr passed away, he sat beside him and made the following statement:

> May God embrace you with mercy, Oh Abu Bakr! By God, you were the first one to embrace Islam! In relation to faith, you were the most sincere, and regarding proximity to God, you had the most profundity. At a time when everyone denied the Prophet, you testified to his Prophethood. When there was no one to help, you brought everything you possessed before him. As everyone remained in their homes, you sat next to him. By God, you were the fortress of Muslims and the nightmare of the non-believers. Your logic and argument has never been feeble, and you have always preserved your brilliant judgment. You have never known the meaning of fear! As the noble Messenger of God indicated, although you were not physically strong, you possessed a faith of steel. Moreover, you were a man of modesty. May we also benefit from your rewards! May God protect us from going astray and losing our way after your departure! [72]

Ali was unsurpassed when it came to bravery and benevolence; however, he also had a matchless personality when righteousness was in concern. One day, he asked those around him, "Who is the most courageous human being?" They replied, "You are, Oh the Ruler of the Faith-

---

[72] Haythami, *Majmau'z-Zawaid*, 9/48.

ful!" "No! It is not I!" said Ali and continued to explain,
"Abu Bakr was the most courageous. During the battle of
Badr, we provided shade for the noble Messenger. When
asked, who would protect the Prophet from the non-
believers, I swear by God, Abu Bakr was the first one who
wanted this mission. He drew his sword and stood guard
over God's Messenger. Without doubt, he was the most
courageous of all men."[73]

Ali loved and respected Abu Bakr so much, and the
feelings were mutual. Abu Bakr always wished to see Ali
by his side, whenever he ran into intricate problems and
complicated issues, he would call Ali and say, "Oh Abu
Hasan! Show us a way out of this!"

When Abu Bakr passed away and Umar became the
new Caliph, Ali was one of the first to pledge his alle-
giance to him. He reserved his seat in the advisory coun-
cil, providing the greatest support for Umar. No one
could be more sincere and openhearted as Ali when offering advice. So much so that one day Umar felt the need to
say, "Without Ali, Umar would have been destroyed!"[74]
Sometimes, when Umar faced complex issues in the
absence of Ali, he would say, "There is a complicated issue
here, but Abu Hasan is not around."[75]

It was Ali who suggested that the beginning of the
Muslim calendar should be marked by *Hijra*, or the Migra-

---

[73] Ibid., 9/47.
[74] Ibn Abdil Barr, *Istiab*, 3/1103.
[75] Ibid., 3/1102–1103.

tion of the Prophet to Medina in 622 CE. Umar accepted his proposal and complimented Ali on his brilliance, "Amongst us, Ali is the most accurate in judgment!"[76]

Following the death of Umar, may God be pleased with him, the gates of sedition and disorder had been opened. Difficult days awaited those who came after Umar. Ali was amongst those who were weeping for Umar. When asked why he was weeping so deeply, he replied, "I am weeping for Umar! His death has opened such a gap in Islam that it would not be closed until the Day of Judgment."

Umar had selected six people as members of a committee that would appoint the next Caliph. Ali was amongst them, and he was also the first member to make his pledge to Uthman, may God be pleased with him.

However, Uthman did not possess Umar's awe and majestic authority. His compassionate and merciful side weighed much heavier. He was like a treasure chamber abundant with tolerance. Unfortunately, this was an opportunity for those who could not raise their voices during the time of Umar to initiate their instigation campaigns. The provocations and seditions began to brew.

All over the city, seditions were popping up like mushrooms. During Uthman's leadership, Ali played an important role in an attempt to stop the negative developments plotted against the Caliphate. Uthman had refused to fight against the rebellions, and Ali was amongst those who believed that he should. As the conflict escalated, Ali placed

---

[76] Ibid., 3/1102.

his sons Hasan and Husayn in front of Uthman's house to guard him against attacks.

Unfortunately, destiny could not be altered, and Uthman's house came under siege. Rebels entered his house and martyred the Caliph as he recited the holy Qur'an.

Ali received the news of his martyrdom from Hasan and Husayn. They were extremely sad because they could do nothing to save him. Ali was furious with them, more furious than they had never seen their father before. If Uthman had been martyred then why were the grandsons of the Messenger of God still alive? Ali shouted at his sons, "If you could not defend him, then you should have died with him!"[77]

---

[77] Tawfiq Abu Alam, *Ahlu'l-Bayt al-Imam Ali*, 91.

WEARING THE GARMENT
OF THE CALIPH

Following the martyring of Uthman, things went from bad to worse. Seditions and conflicts multiplied, casting a dark shadow over the city. These were the times that the noble Messenger had clearly described. Although Ali wished that he could get away from it all, destiny placed the garment of the Caliphate on his shoulders. It was a time when people needed a brilliant leader such as Ali to establish peace. Allah had preserved this brave soul who was raised beside the Prophet to take charge of the leadership of Muslims in such troublesome times.

Ali had been the greatest supporter of the three Caliphs who had served before him, and he had no expectations from the transient world. He released himself into the arms of loneliness, running around like a mad man. He had deep reservations about the future. He was breathing nothing but sorrow. He knew that they would come onto him as their worldly expectations increased. He felt like a carcass...and he had to be prepared for those that prey on carcasses.[78]

---

[78] Abu Nuaym, *Hilyatu'l-Awliya*, 8/238.

However, no one else could put a stop to the ongoing conflicts. When he was considered for the Caliphate position, he tried to remain distant. Unfortunately, neither Talha nor Zubayr nor Sa'd ibn Abi Waqqas or Abdullah ibn Umar would put themselves in for the position he refused. All eyes were searching for him. He could not stay away for too long because it was the congregation Friday prayer, so eventually he had to come to the Mosque of the Prophet. That day, with a unanimous decision, he was selected as the new Caliph of the Muslims. He had no other choice since even the leaders of the community had arrived and had made their pledges to him.

Since this important duty was entrusted upon him, he had to serve in the most appropriate manner. Indeed, it was imperative that Ali fit into the garment of the Caliphate by exerting the necessary effort to keep the banner of Islam raised high.

In reality, rank meant nothing to him, as one judge verified: "Ali had nothing more to gain from the rank of Caliphate. On the contrary, the rank of Caliphate would be decorated with Ali's presence."[79]

Sadly, Uthman's killers were walking freely amongst the people, and a large group concealed their identities. Moreover, they eventually came together as a massive group and stated that they had all done it.

This was an era in which attempts to abolish authority were numerous. The emergence of street gangs was inev-

---

[79] Khatib Baghdadi, *Tarikhu'l-Baghdad*, 1/135.

itable in such conditions of unrest. As the confusion escalated at the headquarters of the Caliphate, the disorder had also spread to the surrounding regions of governance. These regions needed the attention first, so Ali began his leadership by attending to the governors. He appointed new governors to regions where there were noteworthy problems. Those who had been worn out and could not perform efficiently anymore were summoned back to the central administration and replaced by new blood. New governors appointed to Basra, Yemen, Kufa, and Egypt had already begun their services. However, Suhayl ibn Hunayf, who was sent to Damascus, had returned because the previous governor, Muawiya had objected to the new appointment.

This was an indication of tougher days that lay ahead. At first, Ali wrote a letter to Muawiya, inviting him to peace. The prevailing result showed that things were worse than as they seemed. Tears began to flow out of Ali's eyes as he opened Muawiya's reply. There was only a single sentence, which stated, "From Muawiya, son of Abu Sufyan to Ali, son of Abu Talib!"

There was a painful grin on Ali's face as this meant that his Caliphate was not recognized by Muawiya. Soon after, the unfortunate news that came from Damascus was true; Muawiya was preparing a large army and intended to march against the Caliph.

In another region, our mother Aisha was at Mecca with an intention to perform *Umrah* when she had learned of the martyrdom of Uthman. She was overwhelmed by a great sense of sadness. How could the Caliph of the noble Messenger be killed so ruthlessly by street gangs?

Everyone who heard the news had gathered around Aisha. There was great sorrow amongst the Companions. Companions such as Talha and Zubayr had also come to the Ka'ba looking for consolation.

Gradually, paths crossed at Mecca and decisions were made to take revenge from those who had brutally killed Uthman. A large group had gathered and decided to move towards Basra. The intentions were good, but who was going to take control of such a large group?

Meanwhile, following Muawiya's letter, Ali had prepared a large army and marched towards Iraq to restore authority. He had made his preparations assuming that his move may result in a battle. According to Ali, since there was no security at Damascus, he believed that the region was a ticking social bomb that was about to go off.

On the way, he heard of the news that Aisha, Talha, and Zubayr were on their way to Basra with a massive group who wanted revenge. Ali was shocked and froze upon hearing the news. His face had gone pale. Oh my God! What kind of a test was this? Provoking the masses was quite easy, but controlling them was a different story. Large crowds such as these could have easily gone out of control.

Obviously, these people who had left Mecca with good intentions needed to be convinced first. Certainly, Uthman's killers would eventually be apprehended and punished for their appalling crime. However, there was social unrest, and this had to be dealt with first. Ali needed time to restore order. Moreover, there was an existing governing system that would eventually find those who were guilty and punish them. Taking irrational actions may have resulted in catastrophe. Many lives could have been lost. Good intentions were not enough to solve every problem. Sometimes, insufficient information added fuel to the fire.

Analyzing the situation thoroughly, Ali, who was moving towards Iraq to control the potential danger in Damascus, changed his direction and marched towards Basra.

The two large groups met at Zaakar...

BROTHERS TESTED BY BROTHERS

The noble Messenger exerted his efforts to convey the message as it was revealed to him, but he had left Ali to deal with complex issues that would arise in the future regarding the interpretation of the verses. Ali struggled through many troublesome days. He witnessed all dimensions of tests between brothers and made many sacrifices in order to protect the unity of Islam.

On one of these troublesome days, he had been so frustrated that he felt compelled to explain what the noble Messenger thought of him:

> I swear by God who cracks the seeds and cultivates the plants, who distributes the living organisms on the face of the earth, that the noble Prophet promised me this: "Believers will love me and hypocrites will spite me!"[80]

Another time, the noble Messenger mentioned his name at his absence, "Hypocrites are not fond of him and believers do not curse him."[81]

For this reason, some Companions such as Jabir and Said al-Khudri said, "During the time of God's Messen-

---

[80] Ibn Abi Shayba, *Musannaf*, 6/365 (32064).
[81] Ibid., 6/372 (32114).

ger, we would know if a man was a hypocrite or not by watching his behavior towards Ali."[82]

Without doubt, the Owner of all of time and space, who had given the Prophet his mission, had also informed him about the developments that would occur in the future. He knew the issues Ali would face in the future, so he left some important information to certain individuals so that they could deal with difficulties when they arose. This information was to be used as a tool to judge those who sided with Ali and those that rebelled against him in the days of conflict.

Ali had been appointed as Caliph during the days of turmoil and turbulence. He endured many difficulties amid extremes and insufficiencies. The conflicts were not limited to those who instigated seditions, but through instigations and provocations even righteous people with good intentions were being dragged into chaos. It was quite easy to fall into such confusion; Uthman had been martyred, and his killers were not apprehended. Moreover, hundreds of people were claiming that they had killed Uthman.

Ali's job was a difficult one. He also wished to find the killers and punish them, but he needed time. Those who did not possess the patience wanted immediate results, so they developed resentment toward the Caliphate. As the situation escalated with the inclusion of Kharijite rebels, it gave birth to two major incidents of Jamal and Siffin. Looking for the killers of one person had led to spilling of more blood...

---

[82] Ibn Abdil Barr, *Istiab*, 3/1110.

PAINFUL REALITIES AND PARADISE

The Caliph Ali, may God be pleased with him, felt as if his arms had been amputated when he heard the news of the immense crowd (including Aisha, Zubayr, and Talha, may God be pleased with them) that had gathered to seek rapid justice for the murder of Uthman. He said, "Do you know who I am being tested with? Aisha, the most obedient of all human beings; Zubayr, the toughest; Talha, the most genius; and Ya'la, the most cooperative..."[83]

Before long, he sent Ka'ka ibn Amr as a messenger to them. He wanted to convince them as soon as possible since he could predict what was about to develop. Ali had to solve the matter before it escalated to unsolvable levels. Initially, Ka'ka came to Aisha and asked in a kind manner why they had come. Aisha replied, "To establish peace amongst the people!" Then he put the same question to Zubayr and Talha. Their reply was no different. Upon hearing this, he asked all of them, "And how do you intend to manage this?" "By finding and punishing Uthman's killers," they said. Ka'ka had received exactly the answer he was expecting, so he replied:

---

[83] Ibn Hajar, *Fathu'l-Bari*, 13/55.

Let us assume that you killed the murderers from Basra. Will you be in a better situation after you kill these people? In this conflict, you will be killing at least six hundred people and then another six thousand will hit the streets. Whereas, you wish only to punish Uthman's killer, Harkus ibn Zuhayr. However, you will fail to apprehend him because six thousand people are protecting him by claiming to be Uthman's killers. In this situation, shouldn't you give Ali a chance to work things out? Without doubt, he also wishes to punish Uthman's killer, but first he wants to establish order. Then he will certainly apprehend the killer and punish him accordingly.

At this point of the conversation, Aisha intervened and asked, "Tell us your own opinion on this matter, Ka'ka!" "I advise you to remain calm and do not make irrational decisions. Renew your pledges to Ali and become the key figures of peace and righteousness, as you were before. Do not let those instigators of chaos take advantage of the situation," argued Ka'ka.

His speech had been affective, and it seemed the matter was heading towards a peaceful solution. Ka'ka returned to Ali and explained what had happened. Ali became joyous upon hearing the news. He was happy to hear that the problem would be solved without spilling Muslim blood. At that moment, there was no one happier than Ali.

As the situation calmed down at Basra, Ali felt he could turn towards Damascus to deal with the problems there. He ordered his soldiers to prepare for the trip that would commence the next day.

Meanwhile, Aisha and those that accompanied her had come to a region called Haw'ab. They were to camp there, when Aisha noticed something interesting. She came to a complete stop as she heard the dogs barking nearby. She had a puzzled look on her face. Suddenly, she asked, "Where are we?" "Haw'ab," they replied.

Aisha began to tremble upon hearing this reply. Everyone around her was surprised by her reaction, and they all wanted to know why the mother of believers behaved in such an apprehensive manner. They all stared at her regretful face as she spoke, "By God! I am the one he warned about the dogs of Haw'ab!"

No one had any idea of what was going on. They were all waiting curiously for an explanation. Aisha said, "I heard the noble Messenger say to his family members, 'What will happen to one of you when the dogs of Haw'ab begin to bark?'"[84]

In addition to this, according to our mother Ummu Salama, one day the noble Messenger of God indicated that one of his most-pure wives would embark on such a journey. Upon hearing this, Aisha smiled. The noble Messenger then stated, "Beware, Oh Humayra (Aisha)[85]! For this person may be you!"[86]

---

[84] Hakim, *Mustadrak*, 3/129 (4613).

[85] *Humayra* (which means "little woman with a fair, rosy complexion") was an epithet given by the Prophet to his beloved wife Aisha.

[86] Hakim, *Mustadrak*, 3/129 (4610).

His noble words were much clearer now. Aisha had solved the puzzle. This is the reason that Aisha became so agitated upon hearing the barking of the dogs at Haw'ab. She had remembered the noble statement.

She felt shivers going down her spine. "You spoke the truth, Oh Messenger of Allah," she thought to herself. Indeed, this was a day when she heard the dogs of Haw'ab bark, and unfortunately, she was the one who had embarked on such journey.

Could the mother of Muslims ignore such a reality? Certainly not! Immediately, she called Zubayr and quietly mentioned to him that they needed to turn back at once.

However, destiny had other things in store for them. An army was moving towards them. A man on horseback rode into their camp and told them the lie that Ali had come with his army. The man who was assigned to provoke violence was desperately asking for help. He made them believe that Ali's army had ambushed them. In actuality, the group of men who ambushed them was the same thousand men who had been claiming that they had killed Uthman. In the darkness of the night, they thought it was the army of Caliph Ali that had attacked them.

The situation had transformed into a chaotic atmosphere. There was no turning back anymore as the army had approached them. Moreover, there were those who felt they could benefit from such situations. Before long, the news of the similar attacks against Caliph Ali's army had emerged. Suddenly, a chaotic scene appeared at

Jamal. There were clashes, but who was fighting whom? Sadly, brothers who believed in the same God, the same divine Book, and the same Prophet were spilling each other's blood. A community of unity had drawn their swords against each other.

It was a situation in which neither Ali's advice nor Aisha's efforts to establish peace had any effect. Talha and Zubayr desperately tried to put a stop to this terrible conflict, but there was nothing they could do either. Every drop of blood was tearing their hearts apart and every amputated limb was eating them away.

What kind of a test was this? If they refused to draw their swords, they would be killed. On the other hand, if they participated in the clashes, they would be spilling the blood of their brothers.

At this point, Ali risked all to approach his brothers of destiny. They had seemed to be the leaders and only through them this could be solved. Ali shouted, "Talha! Zubayr!"

The two brave souls emerged from the opposite group. First, Ali spoke to Talha, "Oh Talha, how could you leave your family home and take the family of the noble Prophet to battle?"

Friends always spoke the truth, and sometimes the truth hurt. There was nothing to say on Talha's behalf. What sort of a reply could he come up with against such argument anyway?

Ali then turned towards Zubayr, "Oh Zubayr! Remember the day when you were with the noble Messenger and I joined you? You smiled as I walked in, and the noble Messenger asked you, 'Do you love him?' And you replied, 'Yes I do!' Then the noble Messenger had stated, 'Unfortunately, one day you will conduct tyranny against him. You will be in conflict with him, and you will fight against him!'"

Zubayr's world had turned upside down in a matter of moments. This was the power of the word. Everything Ali said was the truth. He replied in humiliation, "You speak the truth! You have reminded me of something that I had forgotten." He placed his sword on the ground and walked away from the battlefield. On the other side, Talha had already made the same decision and walked away from the field.

Another important factor in Talha's and Zubayr's decision to lay down their swords was the fact that they had seen another friend on Ali's side. It was Ammar ibn Yasir. They remembered an important incident that took place during the time of the noble Prophet. One day God's Messenger said to Ammar, "I pity you Ammar! You will be martyred by a rebellious and aggressive group!" This was the day that Ammar stood by the side of Ali. In addition to this, Ali had Hind by his side; he was a person that was raised by the Prophet and had been at the side of the Prophet since the early days of Prophethood.[87] Before

---

[87] Hind was the son of Khadija whom she had from her first husband Abu Hala.

long, Ali found out that just as Ammar, Hind was also martyred. This caused him great sorrow, but he also realized that he stood on the right side; thus he thanked his Lord for granting him this opportunity.

Coming to the battle field was the easy part, but turning back was not so easy. The divine destiny had other plans for both Talha and Zubayr. Zubayr was martyred on his way back to the city by a group of rebels who had ambushed him. A short while after Zubayr's death, Talha became the target of an unfortunate arrow.

It was obvious that their retreat was not taken so lightly by those that fed on chaos. There were no leaders left in the Basra forces. Both Talha and Zubayr had been martyred. The only person they had was Aisha who sat in her compartment mounted on a camel. They encircled her as if they were performing *tawaf* around the Ka'ba. The incident continued to escalate around the camel (from which comes the name of the conflict—the *Jamal* [Camel] Incident.) They were desperately trying to regain their composure. This was a sign of further danger. Quickly, Ali summoned Muhammad, the brother of Aisha. He asked him to take a message to Aisha, proposing that she should be taken to a safe place. The decision would be Aisha's; she had the choice of returning to Mecca or going to Medina. Ali assured Muhammad that the mother of Muslims would be carefully protected. The Jamal Incident was about to end. However, this was a point at which more mistakes could have been made. Therefore, Ali turned to his soldiers and said, "Do not pursue prisoners...show compassion to the wounded, and do not think of collecting spoils. Let us not forget, whoever disarms himself and locks his door shall be in safety today!"[88]

They had received their advice from the Imam. From that point on, gold and silver meant nothing to them. They did not even turn their faces to take a glance. Some of them thought: "If their wealth is not *halal* to us then was it lawful to fight with them?" They could not give any meaning to all the blood that had been spilled. This was the blood of their brothers.

Imam Ali repeated the words, "How could believers become prisoners?" He gave them more reasons to reconsider their situation. Ali taught them a valuable lesson. He was indicating the fact that if Aisha, the mother of Muslims, had also fallen prisoner, who would have the heart to imprison her? This was a contradiction that no one thought of until that moment.

Amr ibn Jurmuz, who had martyred Zubayr—a man whom the Prophet had dubbed as "My Apostle"—came to Ali. He requested permission to enter his quarters. Since he had killed someone from the opposition, he believed that he would be greeted like a hero. He was expecting compliments from the Caliph. Ali roared like a lion, "So you are the one who carries Zubayr's sword!"

Amr was in shock as he was expecting to be praised. He could not understand the meaning of Ali's attitude. Suddenly, Ali took Zubayr's sword off him. First he raised

---

[88] al-Bayhaqi, *as-Sunanu'l-Kubra*, 8/181.

it in the air, holding it with both hands. Then with passion, he held it to his lips. He began to kiss the sword with sorrow. At this point, tears began to flow from Ali's eyes and ran down his cheeks. He said, "The owner of this sword had always protected the noble Messenger against all dangers with passion."

Then with rage, he turned towards Zubayr's killer and shouted, "Oh the killer of Safiyya's son! You shall have your reward in hell!" As Amr left the quarters of the leader from whom he expected compliments, he mumbled, "It is impossible to understand you. I kill your enemy, and you reward me with hell!"[89]

Here Ali had to combat with people whom he had known all his life. Some of them were his dear friends with whom he had shared many difficult days of despair. However, in this situation, the principles of religion came before friendship. Ali's burden was great. He shed tears for those who had given their lives on the opposite side. He attended the funerals of all those he could reach.

---

[89] Ibn Kathir, *al-Bidaya wa'n-Nihaya*, 7/250; Khuzai, *Takhriju'd-Dalalati's-Sam'iyya*, 1/551.

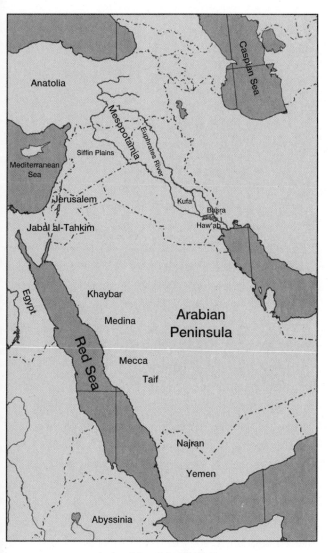

Ancient Map of the Middle East

SIFFIN: THE BATTLEFIELD
OF CONFUSION

Although it resulted in despair, the confusion at Jamal was resolved. Unfortunately, the uproar in Damascus had escalated to dangerous levels. Ali, who had been engulfed with sorrow at Basra, had no other alternative but to march towards Kufa now.

When he arrived at Kufa, they suggested that he move into the palace. Ali refused their offer without any hesitation. This type of worldly temptation formed great stress in Ali's soul, just as it did with Umar ibn Khattab.

Ali was the man of difficult days. Initially, he sought information about public opinion. In order to do so, he constantly walked the streets of Kufa, helping those who needed aid, carrying people's bags, and guiding those who had lost their way. He found great relief in the kind voices of those who recognized him. "Oh the leader of the Faithful!" they would say...before they completed their sentences, Ali recited verses from the Qur'an and helped provide for their needs. Sometimes, he would purchase materials for his own home, and while he carried them through the market, people approached him offering to help. He would refuse, saying, "The father of the house should provide and carry his own rations!"

One day, he had purchased a ladies garment for three Dinars. When he left the marketplace, he seemed like the poor man of Kufa as he rode his donkey through the streets. Some of his men approached him with an offer. They said that they could persuade some of Muawiya's men to join them by tempting them with worldly materials. He declined sternly, "Do you want me to ask for the help of God through deception?"

He was teaching them that the principle of "truth cannot be obtained through deception." He wanted to solve the matter by using negotiators who were respected by Muawiya.

Ali was under great stress at the time. He had left the punishment of those who had murdered Uthman to Allah. All he could do was curse them for causing such a division amongst the believers.

It was a period in which all sincere Muslims wished to avenge Uthman's death. As Ibn Abbas stated, "If people had not wished this, stones would have rained upon us from the sky."[90] This murder of Caliph Uthman was the main factor that laid in the foundation of the current conflicts. There was only one significant distinction, and that was the preferred method of solving the matter. Those who had the weight of the entire Muslim community on their shoulders, like Ali, were making a great effort to

---

90 Ibn Abi Shayba, *Musannaf*, 6/360 (32034).

establish absolute justice by aiming to find the real killers of Uthman and to punish them accordingly. On the other hand, there were those who failed to see the bigger picture, so their perspective was to obtain rapid justice through their own methods as judge, jury, and the executioner. The justice they sought was based on relativity.

There were also those who never carried the burden on their shoulders. They were new Muslims. Ali was a man who lived piety and abstinence from worldly pleasures at its peak, yet he was surrounded by people who lived in riches. These people believed that the days of extreme sensitivity towards *zuhd*[91] were over. Most of these individuals had gathered around Muawiya. Unfortunately, the governor of Damascus had been influenced by them to a certain degree. He believed that he had to act according to the conditions of that era.

In spite of new developments and innovations, Ali never forgot the fact that he was an heir to the values of Prophethood, and he was not about to modify the values he had learned throughout his life. Issues related to religion were practiced perfectly at the beginning, and now they wanted to interpret them the way that was most suitable to them. Ali would not allow religious matters to be the victim of such simple issues. As Ali witnessed these changes in people, he became more involved with absti-

---

[91] *Zuhd* is asceticism or making do with little of this world and leaving what one does not need.

nence and piety. If he was eating two morsels of food a day, he decreased it to a morsel every second day.

As he was extremely sensitive with his private life, he was also exceedingly responsive towards obtaining social harmony. Ali was ready to do everything in his power in the name of peace. This time, he sent Jarir ibn Abdullah to Muawiya with a letter from Ali...

At first, Muawiya interrogated Jarir with his men at Damascus. Then they read Ali's letter with curiosity. The letter summarized what had happened so far and predicted what was about to happen. Unfortunately, this did not convince them either.

The true intentions of Damascus had finally surfaced. They had fixed their eyes on the Caliphate, and revenging Uthman's death was only an excuse. Their tongues spoke of justice and truth, yet they were not aware of the fact that they were heading towards injustice.

In contrast to this, Ali would not permit anyone to talk behind the backs of these people who were his archenemies now. There were two men by the names of Hujr ibn Adiyy and Umar ibn Humk. These two had been talking about Muawiya and the people of Damascus who had been causing problems to Ali. Upon hearing this, Ali sent a stern message, advising them to stop talking behind people's backs immediately.

What kind of manners was this? The people of Damascus were challenging them openly, yet they were not even allowed to talk about them behind their backs. Both of them rushed to Ali and asked, "Oh the leader of believers! Do we not represent righteousness and do they not stand for falsehood?"

It was in Ali's nature to always speak the truth, hence he replied, "I swear by the Lord of the Ka'ba, you are correct!" This was the reply they were waiting for, thus they said, "Then why do you forbid us from talking behind their backs?"

Without doubt, Ali's perspective was different; thus he replied with the following historical words from which we all need to take example: "I do not want you to be back-biters who curse people behind their backs. This is what you should really say, 'Oh God! Protect them and us from spilling blood. Put an end to the conflict that exists between us. Save them from the terrible situation they are in and help them turn away from ignorance. Save them from extremism and let them see the truth!'"

In an attempt to resolve the matter, Ali had sent a personal message to Amr ibn As, who had also sided with Muawiya. Amr was an important person for Muawiya, so Ali believed that Muawiya respected him so much that he would listen to every suggestion made by Amr. But, alas, this attempt to make peace also failed.

All efforts had failed, and there was no other alternative left but to fight. This was not a matter to be taken lightly because brothers were about to go into a battle with each other. In situations such as these, personal views were not important; it was the will of God that had any significance now. That night, Ali gathered his soldiers and said to them, "Beware! You will face the evident army tomorrow. Make the most of your night by offering lengthy prayers and reciting the holy Qur'an. Beseech mercy, forgiveness, and patience from God!"[92]

This was Ali; his attitude during times of war did not vary from his attitude during peace. He advised his soldiers to behave in the same manner.

Finally, Ali heard the news that Muawiya, the governor of Damascus, had left Damascus with his army. There was no turning back now...

The army from Damascus had reached Siffin and took control of the roads that led to the Euphrates River. They planned to deprive Ali's army of water. Nothing could be more heartbreaking than this, not the burning sands of the desert, not the frying rays of the sun, nor the ferocity of the battle. Brothers whom they shared the *qibla* were depriving them of water. Their aim was to weaken them before the battle.

Lips were cracked from dehydration, and not even the great Imam could do anything about it. There was no other option but to solve this issue first. So they attacked those who had blockaded the road leading to the river. The campaign was successful, and the water problem had been solved.

Following their retreat, Amr and Muawiya had the following conversation which summarized Ali's character

---

[92] Tabari, *Tarikhu'l-Umam wa'l-Muluk*, 3/84.

that earned the appreciation of even that of his enemies: "What are you saying Oh Muawiya? What if Ali acted in the way you did and deprived your men of fresh water?" Muawiya said, "Come on Amr! Did you ever think for a moment that Ali would do something like that?" Then Amr said, "Obviously, I do not think Ali would ever do what you have done to him, because he came here for other reasons, not for water."

Finally, the two armies came face to face. Ali still had hope for peace. For this reason only, he sent four of his messengers to Muawiya. They held lengthy periods of negotiations, but they failed to produce a positive result.

Ali had used every means available to establish peace. To his desolation, nothing worked. Eventually, he ordered his men to prepare for battle before sunrise. Some of his men suggested that they attack in the middle of the night to catch the enemy off guard. Ali sternly refused, in the hope that there was still a chance for peace. He gathered his men and made the following speech:

> Do not fight until they attack you first! Praise be to Allah, you are on the path of the righteous. By abstaining from initiating the battle, you will prove this once again. When you attain victory, do not harm those who choose to flee from the battle field. Show compassion to the wounded. Respect those who die on the battle field and refrain from harassment. When you take control of their cities, do not enter their homes without permission. Do not take their possessions... Do not pester their women even if they insult your

leaders and the righteous people... Remember Gold much, so that you may find salvation![93]

The morning had arrived and contrary to Ali's efforts for peace, the battle had commenced. It continued until sunset. That evening, Ali sent another message to Muawiya. He wrote, "Oh Muawiya! Why are we allowing people to die on our behalf? Let us solve this problem one on one. Whoever remains standing shall take control over the leadership!" What a sensitive proposal this was! The caliber of loyalty and self-sacrifice offered by Ali was tremendous...

Upon receiving the message, Muawiya consulted Amr, who suggested, "He is a sensible, compassionate man. Accept his challenge." However, Muawiya knew that those at the battle front would be displeased by Ali's proposal. Realizing this, Amr came up with his own proposal: "Let me challenge Ali on your behalf!" Muawiya did not reply, and this meant that he approved.

The following morning Amr ibn As shouted at Ali informing him that he had accepted his challenge. A combat between the two had begun. Everyone waited impatiently for the result. The fight between the two was most critical because it would establish the winner of the war. The wait in suspense did not last long, for Ali struck and Amr fell off his horse with a thumping noise. Amr was on the ground, and his eyes pleaded for mercy. Although Ali had the right to finish him off, he abstained from delivering the final blow and moved away. Perhaps he remem-

---

[93] Zaylai, *Nasbu'r-Raya*, 3/463.

bered the incident that his beloved brother Usama had
been involved in. Usama had killed a man who had
declared his conversion to Islam. He assumed that the
man converted at the last moment, out of fear of death.
When the noble Messenger had heard about the incident,
he summoned Usama and asked in resentment, "Did you
slash-open his heart to see if he was sincere or not?"[94]

A true wrestler was a person who used his freewill to
control himself in situations in which he had the upper
hand. He had heard this statement from the noble Messenger himself: "A true wrestler is not the one who claims
victory over his opponent, but the one who controls his
wrath in the heat of the moment."[95]

Once before, Ali had again moved away from a person
at a battle field when he had the chance to finish him off.
His opponent had spat on his face. Ali was on the battlefield to please God, not to satisfy his carnal soul...

---

[94] Ibn Hanbal, *Musnad*, 5/207 (21850).
[95] Hannad, *az-Zuhd*, 2/608 (1302).

THE ARBITRATION INCIDENT
AND KHARIJITE EXTREMISM

Ali's sensitivity had given Amr a new soul, but Muawiya's insistent attitude to come up with a new plan to defeat Ali had once again persuaded him. So, Amr had a new strategy, and he explained it to Muawiya: "I had a plan but I reserved it to the last day. You will hold the Qur'an above your head and invite them to its commandment in relation to *tahkim* (arbitration). Whether they accept or refuse, the *tahkim* will certainly form a division and discord amongst them."[96]

When the news reached Ali's ears, he realized that this was a great trickery that would damage the very soul of brotherhood and initiate division and discord among the Muslims. Quickly, he began to warn people.

What kind of a political deception was this? Destruction was so easy, yet construction was so difficult. This was a political maneuver from which he had to seek refuge in God as he did from Satan. Before long everyone had

---

[96] *Tahkim* means to put a dispute between two parties to arbitration in accordance with the Qur'an. In situations of conflict, an arbitrator whose judgment is deemed authoritative would be chosen from both parties to judge and decide the dispute.

heard the seditious news, the spreading of which was far worse than the incident itself.

The division in opinion had already begun to emerge. Disagreements amongst the people were increasing by the minute. Individuals such as Ash'ath ibn Qays and others from the *qurra* (Qur'an reciters) were trying to convince people that it would be healthier to use the Qur'an to pass judgment in this case.

Caliph Ali, on the other hand, was attempting to calm things down:

> I would know the best when it comes to applying the rules of God's Book. However, in this case I know what their intentions are. They are asking for false-hood through righteousness. Did I not go into battle with them for the sake of preserving the principles of the holy Qur'an? How could I even think of turning my back to its principles? Yes, they are holding the Qur'an above their heads and claiming that they wish to apply its justice. This is true, but they are using this to deceive you and to establish chaos amongst you. This is nothing but a trap![97]

The division amongst the people had produced great confusion. No one wanted to fight anymore. They were sick and tired of running from one battle front to another. For this reason only, this seemed like a great solution to them. Muawiya had already appointed Amr ibn As as his arbitrator. As it was known, Amr had a brilliant mind when it came to politics, and he had a reputation for this

---

[97] Ibn Kathir, *al-Bidaya wa'n-Nihaya*, 7/273.

since the time of ignorance. He was very witty and artful, and this had earned him the status of being the man of difficult times. The strategy he had used during his attempts to retrieve the migrants who had travelled to Abyssinia to take refuge in the kingdom of Negus had not been forgotten. He had always opposed Muslims until Hudaybiyah, during which he came peacefully with Khalid ibn Walid to embrace Islam. Ali was well aware of his potential. The day of the Arbitration Incident was inevitable; thus Ali needed someone unique to confront Amr.

A large group headed by Ash'ath ibn Qays insisted that Abu Musa al-Ash'ari should be sent as an arbitrator to confront Amr. However, Ali had his eyes fixed on Abdullah ibn Abbas.

He knew that in this confrontation piety and sensitivity would not be enough. One also needed great wisdom in the worldly affairs. Those who did not have experience in the struggle against the worldly issues would fail against Amr's artfulness. The issue had great importance, since the army they could have easily defeated on the battle field could have attained victory at the table.

Contrary to Ali's view on the matter, the majority ruled, and it was decided that Abu Musa al-Ash'ari would confront Amr at the arbitration.

Following a long period of negotiations at the meeting, a decision was made. They had decided that both Ali and Muawiya were to be removed from their positions. A new committee would be formed to decide on appointing a new Imam.

It was time to announce the decision. Amr invited Abu Musa to announce the decision, and he was to confirm it. This would be the beginning of a period in which a new Caliph would be nominated.

First Abu Musa stepped out and announced that both Ali and Muawiya had been stripped off their duties. Then Amr addressed the people, "As you heard, Abu Musa has removed your own man, Ali from his duty as Caliph. I confirm the removal of Ali from the leadership. I am appointing Muawiya as the new Caliph. He shall take revenge on Uthman's killers. I invite everyone to make their pledge to him!"

These words sent shivers down the spines of all those who had sided with Ali, including Abu Musa. How could unity be broken in such a short time? In contrast to what they had decided during the meeting, Amr made an announcement; he subtly presented the public a fait accompli that would prompt a fresh conflict amongst people. How could they approach such a serious issue so lightly? It was as if they were playing games with the reputation of Caliphate. No one knew who to trust anymore.

Obviously, this meant that they had to return to the battle field. There was no other option because unity had been diminished, and situations were getting out of control. Unfortunately, this was a problem that would not be solved so easily.

As Amr had said to Muawiya when he proposed a solution by the arbitration, the result had formed more confusion amongst the people. The authority of the Caliphate had received a new blow.

Those who claimed that God is the best judge were now abandoning Ali whom they had served for many years. Moreover, some of them had formed a new front against him. This new group provoked the people by asking them questions like, "Is it not disbelief to refute the decision of the arbitration?" Those who replied with "no" lost their heads.[98]

Ali received the news that Abdullah and his wife had been killed by these Kharijite rebels. Abdullah was the son of Habbab ibn Aratt, a precious Companion who had been Ali's beloved friend and a devoted supporter of the Prophet in the early days. Ali was devastated by the news. They had captured Abdullah and his wife and tied their hands to interrogate them. Abdullah was not going to deviate from the truth. First he transmitted a Hadith he had heard from his father. It was a Hadith which explained the exact situation he was in now. The noble Prophet, peace and blessings be upon him, had stated:

> There will be evil seditions! That day, those sitting will be more blessed than those standing, and those standing will be more blessed than those walking, and those walking will be more blessed than those running.

---

[98] This new group that was formed under the name Kharijites ("seceders", literally "those who went out") separated themselves from mainstream Islam. They were a radical, reactionary group who set about creating an ideal society through violence.

It seemed as if these words meant nothing to them as they asked Abdullah about Caliph Ali. "He is blessed!" Abdullah replied. They were not pleased with his answer. So they took Abdullah and his wife to another location. They were both being dragged on the ground. This was quite ironic because on the way they had seen one of their friends eating dates from a tree. They stopped and screamed at him, "How could you eat that date? Have you paid for it or requested permission from its owner? It is *haram*!"

Ironically, these paradoxical people who were extremely sensitive towards religious principles were about to slaughter two Muslims who possessed different views to theirs. Their friend had spat out the date and begged for forgiveness from God.

Before long, they murdered Abdullah, while his wife watched in terror and agony. This innocent woman screamed in pain, "I am pregnant! Fear God, at least for my baby's sake! All her pleas for leniency were in vain. They martyred her just like her husband. Moreover, they had slashed her stomach open and killed her baby as well."[99]

Not long ago, these people were followers of Ali and participated in battles shoulder to shoulder with him. As if what they had done was not enough, they announced that Ali and the opposite side were all in disbelief. It was an incongruous claim. A man like Ali, who had been given already the good tidings of paradise by the noble Messenger himself, was being dubbed as a non-believer. He

---

[99] Shawkani, *Naylu'l-Awtar*, 7/350.

was the beloved son-in-law of the Prophet. He was the master of scholars...The owner of Zulfiqar. The gallant lion of the battle fields was being called an infidel!

This was not a joking matter. The noble Prophet had warned Muslims of such behavior; accusations such as these had always found their target. If the person accused of infidelity was innocent then the accusation returned to its owners. Did not the Prophet foresee everything that was occurring then? He had warned them that one day people would deviate from religion while they ostensibly act in the name of religion.

Before long, the news reached Ali. Oh my God! What kind of a barbaric murder was this? Swords drawn with such fiendish intentions would have destroyed many lives, especially if the perpetrators claimed that they did it in the name of God.

How chaotic the situations were. On the one hand, there was a sacred banner that needed to be carried to the four corners of the world. This was the banner that the noble Messenger had passed on from Hira! On the other hand, there were those who had placed important matters aside to initiate a witch-hunt. Kharijite extremism had taken control over the streets. These people claimed to be Muslims. In their daily lives, they were extremely sensitive towards religious principles. They performed everything according to the judgment of the Book.

However, their tough discipline was not limited to this. They had no knowledge of the worldly affairs and the ever

changing society. This was a result of failing to recognize
necessities and being unable to come up with logical solutions. And the worse of it all was the fact that they believed
they were the only ones who understood the Book.

Ali's blood had frozen in his veins upon hearing the
news. He did not know what to do. Who was he supposed
to fight against?

He was removed from his duty as a Caliph in public.
He could have pulled himself aside and said that situations
did not concern him anymore. His rationale would be that
he was no longer a Caliph in the eyes of the people. He
was just an ordinary citizen amongst the Muslims.

But he could not do this...How could a gallant lion,
who was raised by the noble Messenger himself, stand aside
and watch the destruction of the community from a distance? Without doubt, those who had brought Ali down
today could bring down the Caliphs of the future. Then the
honor of Caliphate would be transformed into a toy which
people played around with as they wished. He remembered
a similar suggestion his son Hasan once made during their
expedition to Jamal when they were about to confront
Zubayr, Talha, and Aisha. Ali then told his son, "If I leave
everything behind and return home, this would be an act of
treachery towards the Muslim community!"

Ali was not the only person who felt extremely uncom-
fortable about the negative developments. There were
other individuals who had refused to join them during the
Jamal and Siffin incidents. They did not wish to fight

against Muslims. One of these people was Abdullah ibn Umar. When Ali summoned him, he said, "I have vowed to God that I would never draw my sword to anyone who recites the words, *La ilaha illallah, Muhammadun Rasulullah* ("There is no deity other than God, and Muhammad is the Messenger of God)."[100]

When Muawiya heard that Abdullah had refused Ali's invitation, he sent a message to him, inviting him to join his front. These were incredible developments. The magnitude of the sedition was immense. Abdullah quickly replied:

> In summary, let me tell you this; I suspect that you wish to draw me to your side because you heard that I have refused to join Ali's army. I swear on my life that I could never reach the profundity of Ali's faith and his immenseness in relation to Hijrah. Also, I could never reach his level of being so close to the noble Messenger and in the gallantry he displayed in battles. Unfortunately, I had made a promise to the noble Messenger in this regards, and this is why I could not join him. So withdraw your hands from me and do not possess false hope.[101]

This great Companion, the son of the noble Caliph Umar ibn Khattab, stated the following words with regret

---

[100] There were many other distinguished Companions such as Abdullah ibn Salam, Usama ibn Zayd, Sa'd ibn Abi Waqqas, Abu Ayyub al-Ansari, Abu Hurayrah and Muhammad ibn Maslama, who had refused to fight against Muslims although they all supported Caliph Ali. See Khalid Muhammad Khalid, *Fi Rihabi Ali*, Daru'l-Maarif, p. 152; Sallabi, *Ali ibn Abi Talib*, p. 468.

[101] Ibn Abdil Barr, *Istiab*, 3/1117.

and tears, "The only thing I regret in my life was not being able to fight besides Ali, against all the evil sedition."[102]

Everything was crystal clear; the noble Messenger had prepared Ali for such difficult days and warned everyone close to him about the future developments. If there was no other proofs for Ali's rightness, Ammar's death at his side would have been enough. Ammar was one of the first Companions who had devoted his life to serving the Prophet, and he was martyred while fighting for Ali. Many years ago, the noble Prophet had pulled Ammar aside and said, "I pity you Ammar! You will be martyred by a rebellious and aggressive group!"[103]

---

[102] Dhahabi, *Siyaru'l-A'lami'n-Nubala*, 3/232.

[103] Hakim, *Mustadrak*, 2/162 (2653).

ALI TAKES REFUGE IN THE
PROTECTION OF GOD

During the days of sedition and social unrest, some decided that Ali's residence should be guarded against possible assassination attempts. Ali saw the men guarding his house and asked why they were standing there. When they told him their intentions, Ali said, "Are you protecting me from those on the ground or from those in the heavens and beyond?"

The Caliph knew that unless the divine destiny above and beyond permitted, no one on earth could have harmed him. However, if it was his time, he would no longer be protected from above and destiny would prevail.

At a time when seditions and confusion had taken control over the people and Ali had decided to resolve the matter once and for all, there were those who refused to take part in the fight. Ali decided to deliver a stern warning to them. In his powerful speech, he said:

> Shame on you! Shame on you! Shame on your attitude which perplexes the mind and shatters the heart! They are on the wrong path, yet they stand in unity. Look at you! You are on the path of the righteous, yet you have fallen apart and you are behaving like

cowards! You have become clear targets and arrows are raining upon you, yet you do not retaliate. They are rebelling to God before your very eyes, yet you do nothing about it…Oh you who only appear to be men on the outside! You are nothing but scarecrows! You resemble those who wear accessories on their feet! By God, you have destroyed my plans with disobedient behavior. You have filled my heart with despair and sorrow…God is my witness that I began to engage in battles when I was only 20. Now, I am over 60. What use is knowledge and experience if no one listens to you? Would anyone believe you even if you possessed a thousand different talents?

AS THE TIME OF REUNION
APPROACHES

On the one hand, he was facing the ruthless seditions of the Kharijites, and on the other, the disunity of his own soldiers. Ali had no other alternative but to return to Kufa. He was in between two fires that were ignited from within. On one side, there were those who used Uthman's death as an excuse to get their hands on the Caliphate, and on the other were those ruthless killers who claimed that they were doing it in the name of God. They were screaming out slogans such as "there is no judgment other than the judgment of God." Ali was surrounded by killers who claimed they were doing it in the name of jihad. Moreover, there was disunity between his soldiers. The spirit of obedience had been damaged by sedition. Ironically, those who insisted that Abu Musa confront Amr during the arbitration were the same people who were accusing Ali of infidelity. That day, contrary to Ali's suggestion of Ibn Abbas, they had pressured him into accepting the representation of Abu Musa.

These unanticipated developments had taken their toll on Ali. Only a person who was raised by the side of the noble Messenger could endure such extreme pressure and rebellion. However, Ali could foresee what was going to happen in the near future. He realized that the end was near. He was pointing at his beard and head when he said, "The color of this beard will turn red with blood rushing down from this head!" A person who heard Ali's comments said:, "If anyone else had stood in Ali's shoes, he would have destroyed the entire family of these murderers." This made Ali upset as he replied, "Fear Allah! I would only request *qisas* on the person who kills me!"

Ali always combined what he had heard from the noble Messenger with the issues he faced and then attempted to find a solution. One day, the noble Messenger had pulled him aside and whispered to him that he would not die of natural causes, but he would be martyred. He had said to him that blood running down from his head would dye his beard red.

On the day of Uhud when martyrs had grown their wings to fly away towards an everlasting life, those left behind had bowed their heads in disappointment. The noble Messenger noticed Ali's disillusionment and said, "Martyrdom waits for you in the future. We shall see your patience on the day when blood rushing from your head dyes your beard red."[104] This meant that Ali would eventually be blessed with the martyrdom he could not attain at Uhud.

On another occasion, God's Messenger asked, "Who were the rebels of the previous tribes?" Ali replied, "Those who slaughtered Prophet Salih's camel." "Then who will

---

[104] Ibn Abdil Barr, *Istiab*, 3/1126.

be the rebels of the future?" asked the Prophet. Ali replied, "I have no knowledge of this, Oh God's Messenger." The noble Messenger then made a gesture with his hand pointing to his neck and said, "They will martyr you in this manner!"[105]

As Ali remembered all this, he lost his appetite. He had submitted himself to the arms of destiny. It was as if he was impatiently waiting for the day that he would join his Lord. He stopped by the home of Hasan and Husayn to have a morsel of food during the predawn meal to fast. When they asked why he was eating so little, he replied, "When my time comes, I do not wish to go to Allah with a full stomach."

He was certain that it was almost time to bid farewell to this world. When we analyze the general information regarding the circumstances in which he was martyred, we realize that he knew exactly the year, the month, the day, and the night that he would be martyred.

He had seen the Messenger of God in his dream and explained to him the difficulties he faced. Even at times when people suggested that he should be cursing the rebels, he opened his hands and made the following prayer:

> Oh Allah! Unite me with Your servants who are more blessed than these. Replace me with someone who can overpower these people.[106]

---

[105] Hakim, *Mustadrak*, 3/122 (4590).
[106] Ibn Abdil Barr, *Istiab*, 3/1127.

On the one hand, he felt joyful knowing that he would reunite with his friends and God, but on the other, he was feeling poignant for what they had done to him. Without doubt, the noble Messenger's heart was also feeling Ali's pain. This conclusion can be derived from the statement of the noble Prophet, who had once said:

> Whoever breaks his heart also breaks my heart. Whoever possesses enmity towards him also bears enmity towards me. When you abuse him, you have also insulted me. Allah loves those who love him and turns away from those who turn away from him. His enemies will also be regarded as enemies of Allah. Whoever submits to him also submits to Allah, and whoever revolts against him also rebels against Allah.[107]

---

[107] Haythami, *Majmau'z-Zawaid*, 9/133.

THE NATURE OF DESTRUCTION
AND MARTYRDOM

U ltimately, a man called Abdullah ibn Muljam from the Kharijites plotted with two of his friends to assassinate Imam Ali. They assumed that this was the only solution. The consequences of their actions had no importance to them. All they wanted was to satisfy their vengeance and abhorrence. They had their eyes fixed on the head of authority. They claimed that it was lawful to spill the blood of a brother in the name of God. They argued, "If we risk our lives to kill the leader who has deviated from the right path, we would be avenging the death of our brothers."

How logical was it to take the life of a believer—especially the *pir* (spiritual guide) of believers—when millions of polytheists were flowing into hellfire? However, it was to be. Once an extremist ideology was formed, there was no way of stopping it from going out of control. They were acting with their emotions. No one calculated the consequences of their actions. They only claimed that they were doing this in the name of God. How could anyone slaughter the Lion of God, in the name of God?

As two of his friends headed towards Damascus to assassinate Muawiya and Amr, Abdullah ibn Muljam came to Kufa with an intention to kill Ali with a poisonous sword he had prepared earlier. No one was aware of his devious intentions. He spent many days planning the attack. He did not want to leave his job to luck.

It was the seventeenth day of Ramadan, a Friday morning. Ali had woken up with the members of his household and prepared for the Morning Prayer. Then he left for the mosque. Although he was still the Caliph, he had no guards to protect him. It was still dark, and he assumed that the person approaching from behind was a worshipper like himself, who was going to the mosque to perform the Morning Prayer. However, Ali was wrong. It was Ibn Muljam. He quickly drew his poisonous sword and began to strike the Caliph from his back.

The gallant hero of the battle fields could have easily overpowered ten Ibn Muljams; however, he wanted his blood to put an end to the constant spilling of Muslim blood. He was heavily wounded and continued to lose blood. As the noble Prophet said many years ago, blood rushing down from his head was dying his beard red. Believing that he had fulfilled his mission, Ibn Muljam shouted passionately, "Oh Ali! Judgment belongs to God, not to you or your friends!"[108]

According to him, he had performed the biggest jihad of them all. Oh my God! What kind of a test was this? This was a series of tests that only Ali could have endured. His concern was not for himself because he was leaving

---

[108] Khuzai, *Takhriju'd-Dalalati's-Sam'iyya*, 1/277.

the hassles of the world behind to join his beloved friends. Only a few days before, he had spoken to the people of Kufa, saying, "I swear by Allah, that I want Him to take me away from here and reunite me with His Mercy!"[109]

Many years ago, the Master of all masters, peace and blessings be upon him, had said to him:

> If one day, people become insensitive towards the afterlife and begin to chase worldly pleasures and temptations...What will happen to you when they begin to value wealth and riches and use the religion of God to deceive others and believe that its preciousness is valid only for certain people?

Ali had replied, "Then I will abandon their world and leave them with their preference. I would choose to be with God and His Messenger in the afterlife. I would persist on being righteous until the day I join you."

This was the day that Ali left their world to them. He was waving to God and His Messenger, asking for permission to come. He had vowed to be patient until death came to him.

Those who heard the news came running to Ali. His wounds were fatal, and they wanted to carry him home. Even in that condition, he said, "Leave me and go perform your Prayer in congregation!"

Ibn Muljam was apprehended. They brought him before Ali. Ali could barely lift his eyelids. He glanced at him and asked, "Are you the man who attacked me?"

---

[109] Ibn Abdil Barr, *Istiab*, 3/1127.

He could hardly speak. There was a sense of deep sorrow in his voice. With one gesture he could have had his head removed, but what kind of greatness was this that he continued to stare at the face of this man with a sad smile. He was about to bid farewell to this life, yet he was still concerned about a chaos that may have occurred following his departure. As blood continued to rush out of his wounds, he looked at the people around him and gave the following advice in relation to his attacker:

> Take him to prison and treat him well. If I live, I will decide on what to do with him. I may forgive him or enforce the judgment of Allah. If I die, I want you to enforce *qisas*, take only his life for my life. Refrain yourselves from damaging his corpse.[110]

Even as he was about to embark on the eternal journey, the great Imam did not want others to be harmed because of his fate as God would not be pleased with those who go to extremes.

Ali was severely wounded as he was brought to his house. A friend named Umar came to his visit. He asked if he could see his wounds. He wanted to boost the morale of the great Imam, as he said, "It is not that serious...I hope you will recover soon."

However, Ali was sure his time had come; hence he was ready to leave for the eternal journey that awaited him. He replied, "Today I am leaving you!"

---

[110] al-Bayhaqi, *as-Sunanu'l-Kubra*, 8/183.

At this point, his daughter Umm Kulthum whom he had wed to Umar ibn Khattab began to scream as she stood behind the curtains. Ali quickly turned towards her and asked, "Why do you weep my beloved daughter? You would not weep if you had seen what I saw!" His friend who stood by his side asked, "What do you see, oh the leader of Muslims?" He said, "There they are…The angels and the Prophets have lined up. The noble master of the universe (peace and blessings be upon him) is speaking to me, 'Oh Ali! The place you are about to go is more blessed than the one you are in now!'"[111]

There was a fragrance that he had kept for many years. It was a souvenir from the noble Prophet. He requested it…he wanted to smell like the noble Messenger of God as he joined him.

By this time, everyone realized that Ali was about to leave them. Before their very eyes, the great Imam was going away to his beloved friends. They did not want further confusion following Ali's departure, so they approached him requesting that his son Hasan, the Prophet's grandson, be appointed as the new Caliph. Ali replied with a "No" at first. Then he said, "I will neither instruct you in this matter nor prevent you from your decision!"

They wished to exert pressure on his conscience. So they said: "What will you say to your Lord when you leave us without a leader?" They were in a difficult situation hence they wanted to confirm the appointment of a new Caliph as

---

[111] Tawfiq Abu Alam, *Ahlu'l-Bayt al-Imam Ali*, 245.

soon as possible. There was no time to waste. The lack of authority meant more confusion amongst the people. However, Ali was certain of his decision as he replied, "I will say to Allah, I came to You as Your Messenger did before, without appointing a new Caliph."

Another day had gone by, and it was Saturday. Ali called his sons, asking them to sit by his side. Perhaps he was about to say his last words to them. He had no energy left in him as he struggled to speak.

He began to give advice to his sons. He told them to fear Allah and never abandon God consciousness and thus act accordingly. He suggested that they should follow Islam no matter what sort of circumstances they faced. He asked them to refrain from disunity and hold onto peace and tranquility as firmly as they could. He suggested that they should always be constructive and that they should always be loyal to the holy Qur'an. He instructed them to be extra sensitive in helping the poor and the needy. He said that they should invite people to Allah and His religion and in doing so, they should ignore those who attempt to ridicule them. He advised them to compete in piety and good manners. Then he said, "The ultimate level of wealth is intelligence...The ultimate poverty is ignorance...The ultimate level of atrocity is arrogance, and the peak of the ultimate munificence is good character and good manners." They asked once again, "What else?" He said:

> Abstain from befriending the ignorant because even
> if he wishes to help you, he will cause you harm.
> Refrain from acknowledging the person known as

liar because he will draw your trusted friends away from you and replace them with those who are distant. Do not endorse the miserly because he will befriend you only to deceive you into believing that he is in need. Do not befriend the dissolute because he will abandon you at the most crucial time.

Then he started reciting the Qur'an and gave his last breath with the following verses:

> Whoever does an atom's weight of good will see it, and whoever does an atom's weight of evil will see it. (Zilzal 99:7–8)

His period of four years and nine months as a Caliph had come to an end. He was sixty-three at the time.

God's Messenger had once said that Paradise was longing for Salman, Ammar, and Ali. Finally, Ali had flown towards the Paradise that impatiently awaited him.

His sons, Hasan and Husayn washed his body and prepared his funeral. Hasan led his funeral prayer, and they carried his blessed body to a location at Kufa. He was buried at the crack of dawn. Curiously enough, the spot where he was buried remains unknown just like the location of the graves of several other important figures.

One day, Ibn Abbas remembered him with tears while he explained:

> He was the husband of the most blessed woman. He was the father of the two grandsons of the Prophet. I have never seen anyone like him, and I will never see anyone like him until the day of resurrection.

He would continue to explain that those who failed to notice his blessedness and tormented him would be the target of God's wrath.

He always had a smiling face. You could see his teeth when he smiled. Since he had never worshipped the idols even when he was a child, they remembered him with the formula of *karrama'llahu wajhahu* (May God honor him) whenever his name is mentioned. Praying for him with this formula had become a tradition. Ali had a unique rank when it came to wisdom, knowledge, piety, compassion, heroism, and benevolence. The attacks initiated against Ali and his blessed family did not stop after his death. The period of evil seditions and provocations continued throughout the lives of Hasan and Husayn. It was an abyss that would also swallow his beloved sons.

THE REPENTANCE OF MUAWIYA

We have to note that Muawiya was also a Companion who had been in the presence of the noble Prophet, peace and blessings be upon him. Although he was not accurate in his decision regarding the ruling (*ijtihad*) on the matter concerning Ali, we cannot continue without giving credit to such a significant soul when the principles of Islam suggest that all those who make *ijtihad* receive rewards even if their decision proves to be incorrect.

Not long after Ali's death, Muawiya held himself accountable for all that had happened. His self-trial on the matter will stand as an example for all believers until the Day of Judgment. Isn't it a fact that we can only prevent history from repeating itself by deriving lessons out of it? A short time after Ali's death, Muawiya was sitting at the rank of the Caliphate. He felt deep sorrow from all that had occurred. However, in order to establish order, they had to have authority. Everyone who had had enough of the conflicts was now coming to Muawiya to make their pledge. Amongst them, there were those who did not join any of the sides during the conflicts.

One of these important individuals who had secluded himself to his house during the conflicts was Sa'd ibn Abi

Waqqas. He was a renowned commander of the front lines whose lips constantly moved to recite sacred prayers. He was one the veteran Companions of the early days. He explained that he had wept only three times in his life; it was on the day that noble Messenger of God passed away; on the day that Uthman was martyred, and on the day that righteousness had taken a blow (referring to Caliph Ali's martyrdom). Then he shouted, "Salam to the righteous!"

One day, Sa'd ibn Abi Waqqas came to visit Muawiya. Muawiya asked him why he had refrained from participating in the battles that commenced with the Jamal Incident. Muawiya said, "Oh Abu Ishaq! You did not approve of our views, but neither were you against us!" It was as if the Caliph was disappointed with him. Sa'd replied:

> Oh the leader of Muslims! Those were the days of darkness. It was so dark that I could not see the end of the road. Then I said to myself, "Sit down and remain where you are." I secured my mount and stayed in my house until the conflicts were over.

Muawiya was an extremely intelligent person. He used his diplomatic wisdom quite efficiently. He replied wisely, "By God, I have read the Qur'an from beginning to the end, and I have not seen a verse that tells you to sit where you are." Then he continued:

> However, I do know that the Qur'an states, "If two parties among the Believers fall into fighting, make peace between them (and act promptly). But if one of them aggressively encroaches the rights of the other, then fight you all against the aggressive side

until they comply with the command of God (concerning the matter). If they comply, then make peace between them with justice and be fair: for God loves those who are fair and just" (Hujurat 49:9). By God! You did not take the side of rebels to fight against those who were just. Neither did you take the side of those who were just to fight against the rebels. You did not even choose to be the one who established peace between the two parties as God had commanded.

Even if Muawiya was the Caliph that day, Sa'd would not refrain from telling the truth. He replied:

You were inviting me to fight against a man, whom the noble Messenger referred to as, "You are to me as Aaron was to Moses. However there will be no other Prophets after me." If you are insisting this much then let me tell you this: I heard the noble Messenger say to Ali, "Wherever you are, you are with the just and justice is with you!"

Upon listening to these, Muawiya asked, "Did anyone else hear this? You must provide evidence." Sa'd replied, "Yes!" and continued, "Such and such person heard it and also Umm Salamah was there."

Muawiya was surprised as he repeated Sa'd's words, "Such and such person and Umm Salamah?"

Our mother, Umm Salamah was still alive hence they came to her for verification. Muawiya said, "Oh the mother of believers! These days, people are assigning words to God's Messenger, yet he has never said such things. Sa'd claims he had heard the noble Messenger say to Ali,

"Wherever you are, you are with the just and justice is with you." What do you say about this?

Umm Salamah thought for awhile and then she took a deep breath and replied, "It was in this house that God's Messenger said those words to Ali."

The situation was serious, and Muawiya had turned pale in the face. You could literally read the regret he felt from his expression. He said:

> Oh Abu Ishaq! From this point on, I will never
> criticize anyone, and I will keep silent in relation to
> Ali. I swear by God, that if I had heard these words
> from the noble Messenger of God, I would have
> never fought against Ali. I would have become his
> servant for the rest of my life![112]

Although he could not undo what had been done, his remorse and repentance was unique. At the very least, Muawiya would have been like a book which is meant to be read, reread, and reflected upon for those that would come after. There were many lessons to be learned from his repentance. He was leaving behind a great example so that others in the future would not make the same mistakes when confronted by similar situations.

---

[112] Haythami, *Majmau'z-Zawaid*, 7/235; Abdur Rahman al-Akk, *Mawsu'atu'l-Uthamai'l-Hawla'r-Rasul*, vol. 1, 361–362.

CONCLUSION

The noble Messenger, peace and blessings be upon him, informs us that a believer will not be bitten from the same hole twice. This advice also tells us that we should not be unrelenting.

Obviously, experience is quite significant here. If we divide the notion of experience into two parts, the first part would be individual experience, and the second part would be social experience. What we can learn from this is that as an individual we can protect ourselves from making similar mistakes while as a society, we should benefit from these historical examples so that we may achieve true peace. Achieving peace depends on our ability to analyze history and carry its significance to our current world.

However, we should never forget to evaluate historical occurrences within their own context and keep in mind the reasons that caused these incidents to eventuate in such manner.

Another reality is that no matter how extensively the historical events are analyzed, there is no way of knowing all the minute details. Those that come after can only pass judgment according to the documents they possess. However, it is impossible to obtain all information regarding a matter that took place many years ago. Sitting at a desk and making judgments about incidents that took place on battlefields would be the greatest tyranny of them all. For this reason, it would be appropriate to leave the judgment to Allah in situations where we lack information.

Experience should be evaluated from this perspective, and when we take a glance at the life of Ali, *karrama'llahu wajhahu*, we realize the importance of the many messages he had left for us. He lived a life at the peak. His life with its good and bad days has a lot to offer. There are many examples and experiences that we can carry into our own social lives.

There is another very significant issue that we are compelled to explain. We have to remember that both sides consisted of the Companions of the Prophet; therefore, it is extremely important that we should refrain from choosing one side over the other. In relation to Ali's example at Jamal, Siffin, or the Arbitration incidents, we should not even bear thoughts such as why didn't they take Ali's side or were they doing the wrong thing by being on the opposite side. The reason for this is that the issue is not limited to individuals, but it concerns a period which involves an entire society. This was a period the people of sedition enjoyed. The conditions had wet their appetite, and they were waiting like hunters who took pleasure out of fishing in murky waters. With every opportunity they had found, they instigated heart-breaking events.

Today, we must not look at the issue from a perspective of who was in the right or who was in the wrong; rather, we should use it as an example to solve current problems.

Otherwise, we would be making a grave mistake by producing assumptions about the other party who were also Companions who sat by the side of the noble Prophet, learned directly from him, and performed their religious obligations ever so sensitively. Carrying the tiniest of question marks in our minds regarding such individuals would be a great deficit on our behalf. As Umar ibn Abdul Aziz said, "As God protected us from those days when believers had blood on their hands or lost their heads to such bloody conflicts, we should also protect our tongues from speaking about them so that our eternal lives are not placed in jeopardy."

Aisha, Zubayr, and Talha, may God be pleased with them, were amongst the most significant Companions. They were all given the good news of paradise while they were living. Also, Muawiya was the perfect scribe of the Revelations. The noble Messenger, peace and blessings be upon him, had once said to him, "If you ever become a leader, rule with compassion."

The noble Messenger had sternly forbidden people from talking negatively about his Companions. He added that those who did had no place in his *jama'ah*. This being the case, we should prevent our tongues from spilling blood. We should remember these Companions with praises and prayers.

The last of the last word would be this; there is no doubt that both parties that consisted of Companions will certainly be taking their place under the *Liwa al-Hamd* (i.e., the "Banner of Praise," which will belong to the

REFERENCES

Abdur Razzak, Abu Bakr Abdur Razzak ibn Hammam; *al-Musan-naf,* (Edition critique by Habibur Rahman al-A'zami), I–XI, Beirut: al-Majlisu'l-Ilmi, 1983.

Abu'l-Faraj, Abdur Rahman ibn Ali ibn Muhammad; *Sifatu's-Saf-wa*, I–IV, Beirut: Daru'l-Ma'rifa, 1979.

Abu Nuaym, Ahmad ibn Abdillah al-Isbahani; *Hilyatu'l-Awliya wa Tabaqatu'l-Asfiya*, I–X, Beirut: Daru'l-Kitabi'l-Arabi, 1405 AH.

_____ *Dalailu'n-Nubuwwa*, [Edition Critique by Muhammad Rawwas Qal'aji, Abdul Barr Abbas], I–II, Beirut: Daru'n-Nafais, 1991.

Abu Ya'la, Ahmad ibn Ali ibn al-Musanna; *al-Musnad,* I–XIII, Damascus: Daru'l-Ma'mun li't-Turas, 1984.

Akk, Khalid Abdur Rahman; *Mawsu'atu'l-Uthamai'l-Hawla'r-Ra-sul,* I–III, Beirut: Daru'n-Nafais, 1991.

Bayhaki, Abu Bakr Ahmad ibn al-Husayn; *Dalailu'n-Nubuwwa,* I–VII, Beirut: Daru'l-Kutubi'l-Ilmiyya, 1985.

_____ *as-Sunanu'l-Kubra*, I–X, Mecca: Maktabatu'l-Dari'l-Baz, 1994.

_____ *Shuabu'l-Iman*, [Edition Critique by Muhammad as-Said Basyu-ni az-Zaghlul], I–IX, Beirut: Daru'l-Kutubi'l-Ilmiyya, 1990.

Bukhari, Abu Abdillah Muhammad ibn Ismail; *Sahihu'l-Bukhari*, I–VIII, Istanbul: al-Maktabatu'l-Islamiyya, 1979.

Dhahabi, Muhammad ibn Ahmad ibn Uthman ibn al-Qaymaz ad-Dhahabi; *Siyar A'lami'n-Nubala*, I–XXIII, Beirut: Muassasatu'r-Risala, 1413 AH.

Dhahabi, Shamsu'd-Din Muhammad Ahmad ad-Dhahabi; *Mizanu'l-I'tidal fi Nakdi'r-Rijal*, [Edition critique by Ali Muhammad

Muawwad, Adil Ahmad Abdul Mewjud], I–VIII, Beirut: Daru'l-Kutubi'l-Ilmiyya, 1995.

Hakim, Abu Abdillah Muhammad ibn Abdillah an-Naysaburi; *al-Mustadrak ala's-Sahihayn*, I–V, Beirut: Daru'l-Kutubi'l-Ilmiyya, 1990.

Hannad, Ibnu's-Sirri al-Hannad; *az-Zuhd*, I–II, Kuwait: Daru'l-Khulafa, 1406 AH.

Haytami, Abi'l-Abbas Ahmad ibn Muhammad ibn Muhammad ibn Ali ibn Hajar al-Haytami; *as-Sawaiqu'l-Muhriqa ala Ahli'r-Rafadi wa'd-Dalali wa'z-Zindiqa*, Beirut: Muassasatu'r-Risala, 1997.

Haythami, Ali ibn Abi Bakr al-Haythami; *al-Majmau'z-Zawaid*, I–X, Cairo: Daru'r-Rayyan li't-Turas, 1407 AH.

Ibn Abdil Barr, Yusuf ibn Abdillah ibn Muhammad; *al-Istiab*, I–V, Beirut: Daru'l-Jil, 1412 AH.

Ibn Abi Shayba, Abdullah ibn Muhammad; *al-Musannaf fi'l-Ahadis wa'l-Asar*, [Edition critique by Kamal Yusuf al-Hut], I–VII, Riyadh: Maktabatu'r-Rushd, 1409 AH.

Ibn Hajar, Ahmad ibn Ali al-Askalani; *Fathu'l-Bari*, I–XIII, Beirut: Daru'l-Ma'rifa, 1379 AH.

_____ *al-Isaba*, I–VIII, Beirut: Daru'l-Jil, 1412 AH.

Ibn Hanbal, Ahmad ibn Hanbal Abu Abdillah ash-Shaybani; *al-Musnad*, I–VIII, Egypt: Muassasatu'l-Qurtuba, undated.

_____ *Fadailu's-Sahaba,* I–II, Beirut: Muassasatu'r-Risala, 1983.

Ibn Hisham, Abdul Malik ibn Hisham ibn Ayyub al-Himyari; *as-Siratu'n-Nabawiyya*, I–IV, Beirut: Daru'l-Kalam, undated.

Ibn Kathir, Abu'l-Fida Ismail ibn Umar ibn Kathir ad-Dimashki; *al-Bidaya wa'n-Nihaya*, I–XIV, Beirut: Maktabatu'l-Maarif, undated.

Ibnu'l-Mubarak, Abdullah ibnu'l-Mubarak ibn Wadih; *az-Zuhd libni'l-Mubarak,* Beirut: Daru'l-Kutubi'l-Ilmiyya, undated.

Ibn Sa'd, Abu Abdillah Muhammad ibn Sa'd al-Mani'; *at-Tabaqatu'l-Kubra*, I–VIII, Beirut: Daru Sadir, undated.

Isbahani, Ismail ibn Muhammad ibni'l-Fadl at-Taymi al-Isbahani; *Dalailu'n-Nubuwwa*, [Edition critique by Muhammad al-Haddad], Riyadh: Daru't-Tayba, 1409.

Khalid, Muhammad Khalid; *Fi Rihabi Ali*, Cairo: Daru'l-Maarif, undated.

_____ *Khulafai'r-Rasul*, Cairo: Daru'l-Miktam li'n-Nasri wa't-Tawzi', 1994.

_____ *Rijalun Hawla'r-Rasul*, Beirut: Daru'l-Kitabi'l-Arabi, 1987.

Khatib Baghdadi, Ahmad ibn Ali ibn Abu Bakr; *Tarikhu'l-Baghdad*, I–XIV, Beirut: Daru'l-Kutubi'l-Ilmiyya, undated.

Khuzai, Ali ibn Mahmud ibn Suud al-Khuzai; *Takhriju'd-Dalalati's-Sam'iyya*, Beirut: Daru'l-Gharbi'l-Islami, 1405 AH.

Mizzi, Yusuf ibn az-Zaki Abdur Rahman Abu'l-Hajjaj al-Mizzi; *Tahzibu'l-Kamal*, I–XXXV, Beirut: Muassasatu'r-Risala, 1980.

Mubarakfuri, Abu'l-Ula Muhammad Abdur Rahman ibn Abdir Rahman ibn Abdir Rahim al-Mubarakfuri; *Tuhfatu'l-Ahwadhi*, I–X, Beirut: Daru'l-Kutubi'l-Ilmiyya, undated.

Muslim, Abu'l-Husayn al-Hajjaj an-Naysaburi; *Sahih Muslim*, I–V, Beirut: Daru'l-Ihyai't-Turasi'l-Arabi, undated.

an-Nasai, Abu Abdir Rahman Ahmad ibn Shuayb; *as-Sunan*, [Edition critique by Abdul Fattah Abu Ghudda], I–VIII, Aleppo: Maktabatu'l-Matbuati'l-Islamiyya, 1986.

_____ *as-Sunanu'l-Kubra*, [Edition critique by Abdul Ghaffar Sulayman al-Bundari], I–VI, Beirut: Daru'l-Kutubi'l-Ilmiyya, 1991.

al-Qurtubi, Muhammad ibn Ahmad ibn Abu Bakr ibn Farah; *al-Jami' li Ahkami'l-Qur'an (Tafsiru'l-Qurtubi)*, I–XX, Cairo: Daru's-Sa'b, 1372 AH.

Sallabi, Ali Muhammad Muhammad as-Sallabi; *Asma'l-Matalib fi Sirati Amiri'l-Mu'minina Ali ibn Abi Talib: Shahsiyyatuhu wa Asruhu*, Alexandria: Daru'l-Iman, undated.

Shawkani, Muhammad ibn Ali ibn Muhammad as-Shawkani; *Naylu'l-Awtar Sharh Muntaqa'l-Akhbar*, I–IX, Beirut: Daru'l-Jil, 1973.

Tabarani, Abu'l-Qasim Muhammad ibn Ahmad; *al-Mu'jamu'l-Awsat,* [Edition critique by Hamdi ibn Abdil Majid as-Salafi], I–X, Cairo: Daru'l-Haramayn, 1415 AH.

_____ *al-Mu'jamu'l-Kabir*, [Edition critique by Hamdi ibn Abdil Majid as-Salafi], I–XX, Mosul: Maktabatu'l-Ulum wa'l-Hikam, 1404 AH.

_____ *al-Mu'jamus-Saghir*, [Edition critique by Hamdi ibn Abdil Majid as-Salafi], I–II, Beirut: al-Maktabatu'l-Islami and Amman: Daru Amman, 1985.

Tabari, Muhammad ibn Jarir ibn Yazid ibn Khalid at-Tabari; *Tarikhu'l-Umam wa'l-Muluk* (*Tarikhu't-Tabari*), I–V, Beirut: Daru'l-Kutubi'l-Ilmiyya, 1407 AH.

Tawfiq Abu Alam, *Ahlu'l-Bayt al-Imam Ali*, Cairo: Daru'l-Maarif, 2003.

Zaylai, Abdullah ibn Yusuf Abu Muhammad az-Zaylai; *Nasbu'r-Raya*, I–IV, Egypt: Daru'l-Hadith, 1357 AH.